THE
IMAGE
OF
GOD

THE IMAGE OF GOD

GLENN SUNSHINE

EVERY SQUARE INCH PUBLISHING

Every Square Inch Publishing
www.esquareinch.com

ISBN-13: 978-0-9892692-0-9

To Paul, David, and Flo Abel,
who many years ago
got me started thinking
about worldview.

TABLE OF CONTENTS

INTRODUCTION

QUESTIONS

- What does it mean to be human?

- Is there such a thing as human rights? If so, what are they?

- How can we say that all people are equal when some are more intelligent, more athletic, better looking, wealthier, or have more opportunities than others?

- Does work have any meaning beyond making a living?

- How should human beings relate to the environment?

- Are we different from animals?

- What is marriage? What is family?

- Does sex have any deeper meaning beyond personal pleasure?

- Why is the world so messed up?

- Is there any solution?

- What is the meaning or purpose of life?

    So many questions ....

GOD'S DEFINITION

The answer to all these questions and more are embedded in the answer to the first question, what it means to be human. For Christians, the place to find the answer is in the Bible. In the first chapter of Genesis, when God consults with Himself about creating humanity, He gives His definition of what it means to be human: "Let us make man in our image, in our likeness" (Gen. 1:26a).

The first thing God says about humanity is that we are made in His image. Everything about what it means to be human flows from there. This concept has enormous implications for our lives, for our culture, and for society, yet we hardly ever talk about it. There was a time when the church understood this, in those bygone days when Christians believed that they should lead the culture rather than follow it. Until fairly recently, Christians worked to apply the biblical understanding of what it means to be human to the full range of human experience. The result was the transformation of work, the development of technology, the rise of science, the idea of human rights, the abolition of slavery, improvement in the status of women, promotion of monogamy, the creation of great art, and a host of other elements that shaped Western civilization and created the modern world.

Unfortunately, we've largely forgotten all that, and so has our culture.

THE AWOL CHURCH

American society has lost sight of the meaning and purpose of human life. We give lip service to supporting people with disabilities, but when we find them we exterminate them in utero. We idolize sex yet have divorced it from its biological purpose. We have made children a lifestyle accessory available to pretty much everyone who wants one. So-called same sex marriage is increasingly considered an obvious human rights issue when it did not even exist anywhere in history prior to

2001. We view work as either a necessary evil rather than a positive good, or we idolize it. We have a consumerist mentality that says that Jesus was wrong and that life does consist in the abundance of our possessions. Young people live vicariously through video games rather than doing something with their lives in the real world. Contemporary art celebrates meaninglessness. More people are enslaved today than at any point in human history.[1] The list is endless.[2]

The need in our society is thus great. The challenges raised by bioethics alone should drive us to examine what the Bible says about what it means to be human. Unfortunately, the church has not taught a message that is capable of addressing the unprecedented cultural changes that we are facing.

Liberal churches have largely adopted an agenda indistinguishable from liberal politics. They have thus made themselves irrelevant: if I can do the same things and work on the same causes through a Political Action Committee, what do I need the church for? Conservative churches have reduced Christianity to the message of salvation, and the Christian life to "spiritual" activities (typically limited to prayer, Bible study, going to church, and evangelism) plus morality. These churches have essentially nothing to offer to the culture. Personal salvation, yes; cultural impact, no.

But Jesus tells us that we are the salt of the Earth and the light of the world. If our culture is decaying and becoming dark, it is because we are not doing our job. And a big part of the reason we are not doing our job is we don't understand the fullness of the Gospel, and that Christians are meant to be bring the Kingdom of God to bear on every area of life and culture.

In other words, we don't understand the image of God and its role in developing an integrated vision of life. We need

1   See, for example, E. Benjamin Skinner, *A Crime so Monstrous: Face to Face with Modern Slavery* (Free Press, 2009).

2   How we have reached this state of affairs is discussed in my book, *Why You Think the Way You Do* (Zondervan, 2009).

to re-learn the idea that all legitimate work is a calling from God, that the work of the scientist, the artist, the teacher, and the auto mechanic is just as spiritual as the work of the pastor because all of these jobs can and should be done to the glory of God and the good of our neighbor. Once we understand that, the Gospel becomes far bigger than personal salvation, as important as that is. Rather, it offers a positive vision of culture, a good and compelling picture of the way things are supposed to be. Rather than being sellers of fire insurance, we have good news both for this world and for the next.

This brief study cannot cover all of this in any detail, but the core of that cultural vision has to be a recovery of the full-orbed picture of what it means to be made in the image of God. Understanding this will help us navigate through the maze of issues raised by science and technology that are advancing faster than our ethics. It will help us recover the rich tradition of the arts where Christians once excelled. It will guide us through the social and cultural challenges that our society is throwing at us. And it will provide a firm foundation for continuing with the unfinished task of promoting human rights and freeing the slaves. In other words, it will give us a solid biblical foundation for addressing the issues we face.

If you are reading but are not a Christian or do not accept the authority of the Bible, I'd encourage you to read it with an open mind. It will help you understand the impact the Bible has had in shaping Western culture, and it will present ideas you probably have not heard before. Who knows, you may even find them compelling.

With that said, let's get started.

O N E

THE IMAGE OF GOD
AND STEWARDSHIP

TO BE HUMAN

One of the most important statements in Scripture about what
it means to be human occurs in the very first chapter of the
Bible:

> *Then God said, "Let us make man in our image, in our*
> *likeness, and let them rule over the fish of the sea and*
> *the birds of the air, over the livestock, over all the earth,*
> *and over all the creatures that move along the ground."*
>
> *So God created man in his own image, in the image of*
> *God he created him; male and female he created them.*
> —Gen. 1:26-27

Although this is the essence of the Biblical definition of
humanity, it is frequently ignored, misinterpreted, or given
little real consideration by contemporary Christians. Misun-
derstanding this point leaves us with little practical foundation
for understanding the multi-faceted responsibilities God has
given us in this world.

Before exploring what the image of God is, it will be help-
ful to clear up some misconceptions that come from failing to
understand the use of the phrase "image of god" in the ancient near east.

◆ The image of God is not, as some liberal scholars have suggested, an explanation for anthropomorphic deities (i.e. gods who look like humans). Aside from getting things backward—if anything, the term describes humans as "theomorphic" (God-shaped) rather than God as anthropomorphic (human-shaped)—this idea misses the point of what the phrase was trying to convey. It says nothing about God, and everything about humanity and our responsibility to God.

◆ The image of God is not found in human beings having a body like God's, as the Mormons teach. This again misses the point. Scripture is clear that God is Spirit (Jn. 4:24) and the only body He has is Jesus'. This is why the second commandment bans the use of images in worship: by their very nature no image can convey the essence of an invisible, non-corporeal being. Images thus conceal more than they reveal and they can encourage us to think of God as less than and other than what He has revealed Himself to be. Yes, Scripture describes God as having arms, eyes, and ears. But these are metaphors to convey His ability to know and act in the world and do not tell us that God actually has a human-like body any more than the passages that say we are sheltered under His wings suggest that God is a heavenly chicken.

◆ The image of God is not a form of idolatry, as Islam teaches. Mohammed grew up in the world of Arabian paganism, where idols were everywhere. In his move to monotheism, he rightly recognized that God does not have a body and so Islam absolutely banned any images of Allah for fear that they would lead people back to paganism and idolatry. Like the second commandment, Islam also argues that any representation of God is by nature false. So far, so good. But Mohammed and his followers did not understand the significance of the phrase "image of God" in its cultural context. It does not refer to anything idolatrous.

Ironically enough, its principal meaning is not very different from Islam's understanding of the place of humans in the world.

So what did the phrase, "image of a god" mean in the ancient near east? To answer that, we need to know something about the history of the area. In the Mesopotamian world, life was unpredictable and precarious. The area was subject to erratic and destructive flooding and was open to invasion. It is no wonder then that the city states were literally built around religion: the center of every city was a ziggurat, a temple to the city's major deity, and priests dominated the civilization, at least initially.

Over time, a power struggle ensued between warlords known as ensi and the priests. In an effort to legitimize their authority in these highly theocratic societies, the ensi associated themselves with the gods, claiming to be their official regents and representatives to the world. This enabled them to emerge as kings with a credible claim to rule over the priests. These kings were commonly referred to as the images of a god: they were that god's "face" in this world, which is what gave them the right to rule.

ROYAL AUTHORITY!

By designating humanity the image of God, Genesis conveys royal authority on us. This idea is further reinforced by the language in the rest of Gen. 1:26. In Hebrew, when you want to emphasize something, you repeat it. Thus the angelic beings in Isaiah 6 and Revelation 4 declare God to be "holy, holy, holy." Similarly, Hebrew poetry is characterized by "parallelism," the repetition of an idea in different words. This can be seen in Ps.19:1-2:

> *The heavens declare the glory of God;*
> *the skies proclaim the work of his hands.*
> *Day after day they pour forth speech;*
> *night after night they display knowledge.*

The indented line repeats the same idea as the previous line in different words. That's parallelism at work.

In Gen. 1:26, for the first and only time in the creation story, God consults with Himself about something He is about to create. The pronouncement He makes thus highlights the fact that something special is about to occur, and as is suited to the occasion, the language is heightened by a kind of parallelism similar to Hebrew poetry. God says He is going to create humanity in His image, and then elaborates on what that means by indicating that we are to have "dominion" over fish, birds, livestock, and all the earth.

At this point, a lot of Christians get nervous, because we know from history how tyrannical royalty can be. "Dominion" easily turns into domination and abuse. And in fact, Christians have been regularly accused of using this verse as an excuse for everything from strip mining and plundering resources to pollution.

In response, we must recognize that in the ancient near east, royal authority came from a god and thus was exercised in the god's name and under the god's authority. This is especially true in Genesis. True, we are given authority, but it is the authority of a steward, not of an independent monarch.

The Lord of the Rings (the book more than the movie) illustrates the difference well. The Stewards of Gondor have absolute authority to rule the city in the absence of the king, protecting it and holding it until such time as the king returns. Denethor makes it clear to Boromir that they can never become kings, because that is not their place. If or when the king returned, the stewards were to return their stewardship to him and were to be judged for the faithfulness with which they carried out their duties. As 1 Cor. 4:2 puts it, it is required of stewards that they be found faithful.

In the same way, the earth is the Lord's, not ours (Ps. 24:1). We may have dominion, but it is only the dominion of a steward, carrying with it the responsibility to pass on a carefully tended and protected world to our heirs and to Christ when He returns.

This is not a new understanding of our environmental responsibilities. For example, John Calvin, who is regularly (and wrongly) vilified as providing the theological justification for out of control capitalism and the accompanying exploitation of the environment, had this to say in his commentary on Gen. 2:15:

Let him who possesses a field, so partake of its yearly fruits, that he may not suffer the ground to be injured by his negligence; but let him endeavour to hand it down to posterity as he received it, or even better cultivated. Let him so feed on its fruits, that he neither dissipates it by luxury, nor permits [it] to be marred or ruined by neglect. Moreover, that this economy, and this diligence with respect to those good things which God has given us to enjoy, may flourish among us; let every one regard himself as the steward of all things which he possesses. Then he will neither conduct himself dissolutely, nor corrupt by abuse those things which God required to be preserved.[1]

In his sermon on Gen. 2:7-15, Calvin adds that whether rich or poor, we must remember that whatever we have, we are to use it with the sure knowledge that one day, we will have to give an account to God of what we have done with the things He has entrusted to us.[2]

A Question of Stewardship

The historical Christian tradition has thus been committed to environmental stewardship, recognizing that though we have authority on earth, we also have great responsibility to use and develop the world as caretakers of God's possession. We

1   John Calvin, *Commentaries on the First Book of Moses Called Genesis*, translated from the original Latin and compared with the French edition, by the Rev. John King, vol. 1 (Edinburgh: Calvin Translation Society; reprinted Grand Rapids: Baker, 2005), 125.

2   Jean Calvin, *Sermons sur la Genèse*, Chapitres 1,1-11,4, ed. Max Engammare (Neukirchen-Vluyn: Neukirchener Verlag, 2000), 108-109.

cannot fall into the trap of worshipping the world, as both ancient and modern paganism has done, but we cannot neglect
our responsibilities either.

In the first instance, the image of God refers to humanity
as royalty, appointed by God as His representatives, regents,
and stewards over creation. This gives us enormous responsibilities, but also dignity and the right to enjoy the creation.
It also establishes the only firm foundation for the idea of
universal human rights, the subject our next chapter.

QUESTIONS

1. Read Gen. 1:26. What does it mean to you that God created humanity in His image? Have you ever given any thought to what that says about you and about God?

2. What does the concept of human beings having dominion over the world mean to you? Do you see this as a positive or a negative?

3. In 1967, historian Lynn White, Jr., wrote an essay entitled "The Historical Roots of Our Ecological Crisis." This essay argued that the Bible's teaching on human dominion was responsible for the environmental degradation that was a growing concern in the 1960s. This argument has now become a staple of the environmental movement. Do you think the Bible teaches a kind of dominion that can lead to environmental degradation and abuse? Why or why not?

4. Read Lev. 25:23, Deut. 10:14, Ps. 24:1, and Job 41:11. What do these verses add to your understanding of the nature of humanity's dominion over the earth?

5. Stewardship is defined in the Holman Bible Dictionary (1991) as "Utilizing and managing all resources God provides for the glory of God and the betterment of His creation." Do you think this definition successfully balances God's authority and humanity's dominion? Why or why not?

6. What resources (e.g. time, talent, treasure, truth, relationships) has God entrusted to your stewardship? How are you doing in your stewardship of them? Which areas do you need to pay more attention to?

The Image of God

T W O

THE IMAGE OF GOD
AND HUMAN DIGNITY

GOD'S REP

In the first chapter, we saw that the phrase "image of God" was a royal term that described humanity as the official representative and regent of God in this world. This leads to the biblical teaching of human dominion over nature, but at the same time limits that dominion to acting as God's steward in the world and taking care of it appropriately as His possession.

Since in Genesis 1, the description of humanity focuses entirely on the image of God, it follows that this is the most essential element of what it means to be human. But this in turn has implications well beyond dominion and stewardship. In particular, it provides the only real foundation for human dignity and human rights.

DIGNIFIED ABOVE ALL ELSE

First of all, the image of God distinguishes us from everything else in creation. Spain may grant "human rights" to great apes[1] and Switzerland may have enshrined "plant rights" into its constitution[2], but neither of these alters the fundamental distinc-

---

1   http://www.guardian.co.uk/world/2008/jun/26/humanrights.animalwelfare.

2   http://www.weeklystandard.com/Content/Public/Articles/000/000/015/065njdoe.asp.

tion between humans and either animals or plants. In fact, they demonstrate the difference: has any other species given rights to anything else? Has any other species acted to protect other species? Has any other species held itself in check in an effort to prevent another species from extinction?

The very fact that we can talk about rights and that we recognize our responsibilities toward other creatures puts the lie to the claims of animal rights activists that we are just another species on the planet, no different from any other. If that's the case, why do they insist that we must protect and respect other species? If they don't ask that of termites in a house, which destroy our habitat, or a lion meeting a lone wildebeest, why do they expect it of humans? Or should we put predatory animals in jail?

We do in fact have responsibilities to other creatures, and for that reason the animal and plant rights activists who deny a special place for humans are wrong. It is precisely our creation in the image of God that gives us those responsibilities and that distinguishes us from the rest of Creation. The claim that this outlook is "speciesism," a moral failing akin to racism, is self-refuting unless those leveling the charge are also willing to say that all other species have the same responsibilities—not just rights—that we do.

Christians have supported an appropriate form of animal rights for centuries. For example, William Wilberforce, the British evangelical who led the fight in Parliament against the slave trade, also was a founder of the Society for the Prevention of Cruelty to Animals. But equating animal rights to human rights is a different issue altogether, and points to a fundamental deterioration in our culture's understanding of and commitment to the value of human dignity, and with it, to human life itself.

THE IMAGE OF GOD
AND THE VALUE OF LIFE

In Biblical terms, humanity's unique dignity flows from our creation in God's image. Since we are God's regents on the earth, an attack on any human being is tantamount to an attack on God Himself. Thus God tells Noah after the Flood:

> *Whoever sheds the blood of man,*
> *by man shall his blood be shed;*
> *for in the image of God has God made man.* —Gen. 9:6

The justification in this instance for capital punishment was the fact that human beings are made in God's image. Murderers forfeited their right because of their attack on one of God's image bearers. That is how seriously God takes human life.

Taking this one step further, since the value of human life flows from the image of God, so does human dignity. And since the image of God is shared by all people, all of us have an intrinsic dignity that is distinct from anything else about us. The supreme value of the image of God far outweighs any other consideration in determining our worth.

INSULTING GOD?

To put it simply, any time you value something more than the image of God in how you think about yourself or others— whether race, sex, class, appearance, age, mental capacity, ability, disability, *anything*—you are quite literally insulting God to His face.

This includes valuing people on the basis of their religious beliefs. Christians who think they are better than others because of their faith have forgotten a fundamental element of the Good News: we are all sinners who can bring nothing good to God that would make us worthy of salvation. But what we could not provide for ourselves, God provided for us, and the fact that we are Christians says more about the mercy and grace of God than it does about us. Christians thus have no claim to being better than anyone else, and we must insist that all human beings are equally valuable regardless of faith, lifestyle, vices, criminal background, or anything else, because we all share the image of God.

There is therefore never any excuse for any form of bigotry, whether racism, sexism, classism, ageism, ableism, or any of the other "-isms" of our culture. As a result, Christians should be (and historically have been) on the forefront of fights for civil rights.

THE IMAGE OF GOD AND HUMAN EQUALITY

From its earliest days, Christianity has argued for human equality before God. The apostle Paul tells us that in Christ, "there is neither Jew nor Greek, there is neither slave nor free, there is neither male nor female." (Gal. 3:28 ESV) All are morally and spiritually equal before God, all equally need salvation, and all share in the same means of salvation. Race, class and gender thus are irrelevant before God.

This emphasis on moral and spiritual equality led Christians to be the first people anywhere in the world to pass laws against slavery, as documented by Rodney Stark, sociology professor at Baylor University.[3] Slavery was condemned as a sin in Aquinas's *Summa Theologica*, and when the Europeans tapped into the African slave trade, no fewer than four different popes condemned it.[4] And of course, the British abolition campaign in the late 1700s was led by evangelical Christians, among them William Wilberforce.

Martin Luther King's leadership in the Civil Rights movement was based on a profound understanding of Christian natural law theory going back at least as far as Thomas Aquinas in the early thirteenth century. King's *Letter from Birmingham Jail* is based on just these arguments, anchored in the Christian tradition that recognized both our equality and intrinsic dignity and the importance of an objective moral foundation for law.

Early Christians promoted the rights of children and the unborn as well. In the Roman era when infanticide was

---

3   *Victory of Reason*, 29-31.

4   Ibid., 200-202.

mandated by law for the handicapped and allowed under any circumstances, Christians saved babies from death, bringing them into their own households, and petitioned the government to end this legalized murder. Similarly, following the lead of the Jews, they also opposed abortion as murder since it was the taking of a human life made in the image of God.

Christians pioneered rights for women as well. Christianity resulted in a tremendous increase in prestige, opportunity, and freedom for women in ancient Rome, well beyond what had been available to them in the pagan world.[5] We will return to this topic in a later chapter.

Ultimately, the logic of our creation in the image of God led to the development of the idea of universal human rights. This is a uniquely western concept, built on theories of unalienable rights developed by Medieval Christian theologians from their studies of the Bible. And all of it is founded on the spiritual and moral equality of people in Christ, going back ultimately to our creation in the image of God.

No other culture, religion, or civilization has advanced a comparable idea, because none of them have the worldview foundation for it. Even Jürgen Habermas, the leading public intellectual in Europe and an atheist, points out that modern secular ideas of human rights have their origins in the Judeo-Christian tradition, and though secularists can appropriate these ideas, denying their foundation is intellectually dishonest:

> *Egalitarian universalism, from which sprang the ideas of freedom and social solidarity, of an autonomous conduct of life and emancipation, of the individual morality of conscience, human rights and democracy, is the direct heir of the Judaic ethic of justice and the Christian ethic of love. This legacy, substantially unchanged, has been the object of continual critical appropriation and reinterpretation. To this day, there*

---

5   Rodney Stark, *The Rise of Christianity*, 95-128.

is no alternative to it. And in light of the current challenges of a postnational constellation, we continue to draw on the substance of this heritage. Everything else is just idle postmodern talk.[6]

All of this obviously just scratches the surface of this issue. But in an era of easy abortion coupled with ultrasounds and genetic testing to determine if the child is worth keeping alive, of designer babies, of calls for legalized euthanasia, and a host of other challenges to human life and worth in our culture, we as Christians need to rediscover and recommit to the centrality of the image of God for determining human value.

---

6   *Time of Transitions,* 150.

QUESTIONS

1. Read Ps. 8. What does it tell you about human dignity?

2. What is the basis of your own self-image? How does your creation in the image of God factor into it?

3. How does our responsibility to be God's stewards in the world affect our ideas of animal and plant rights? How do those rights differ from our rights as image-bearers of God?

4. Read Gal. 3:28 and Col. 3:11. What do these verses tell us about human equality before God?

5. Are there any groups or persons in whom you have a hard time seeing the image of God? Are there any groups that you see as being more valuable than others? How should our common creation in the image of God affect how you think about these groups?

6. We live in a world where rape, torture, genocide, and murder happen. How do we reconcile the idea that even the people who do such things are created in the image of God, with the demands of justice and our very natural revulsion for their actions?

7. What is the connection between the image of God and human rights? Medieval theologians found unalienable rights in Scripture. Can you think of any biblical passages that support the idea of either human rights in general or specific rights?

THREE

The Image of God

THE IMAGE OF GOD AND GENDER

FROM THE BEGINNING

In the first two chapters of this book, we have seen that the image of God refers to humanity's dominion over the world as God's stewards, and that it is the basis for the unique dignity of human beings, for equality, and for human rights. In this article, we will look more closely at the issue of gender.

Gender is specifically mentioned in the first passage in Scripture dealing with the image of God: ... *So God created man in his own image, in the image of God he created him; male and female he created them. —Gen. 1:27*

Notice that the text very pointedly identifies the image of God with both male and female. Men and women are thus equally image bearers of God, and this means that they are intrinsically equal in worth, in their rights, and in their call to exercise dominion in God's name over the earth.

It is impossible to overstate how revolutionary this idea was in the ancient world. We sometimes hear the argument that paganism is far better for women than monotheism, because in paganism there are goddesses along with gods, thus providing women with a claim to status and even authority in society. This argument is great in theory. In practice, it's total nonsense.

Women under paganism

In the real world, paganism almost inevitably placed rigid restrictions on women's roles. Essentially, they were only permitted to do things that the goddesses did. And generally speaking, this meant that they were responsible for the domestic sphere and often little else.

In Greece, for example, "free" women did not leave the home even to go shopping—that was handled by the men or by slaves. In places like Ephesus or Corinth that were dominated by temples to goddesses, the priestesses had more public roles, but they also doubled as prostitutes. And in general, only a very small number of wealthy women, priestesses, and prostitutes had any roles or responsibilities in public life.

Further, women were considered intrinsically inferior to men in almost all ancient cultures. Aristotle, for example, considered women to be essentially the result of birth defects—they were "misbegotten men," incomplete and inferior physically, morally, and intellectually.

Women also were not valued as highly as men, an attitude that persists in many parts of the world today. In Rome, wives came in a distant third for their husbands, behind parents and sons. As for children, Romans typically kept all healthy boys and their first daughter; the rest were discarded and left to die.

And these problems were not limited to the Greco-Roman world. All major civilizations in the ancient world and the vast majority of minor cultures held women as distinctly inferior to men, with far fewer rights, privileges, or opportunities.

Judaism

Things were quite a bit different in Judaism, largely due to Genesis 1:27. Women were seen as being equal to but different from men because of their common creation in the image of God.

Spiritually, women were seen as setting the tone for the entire family, so much so that it was believed that a pious man who married an evil woman would become evil, and an evil man who married a pious woman would become pious. Women were seen as more intuitive than men, and some scholars argued that the wives of the patriarchs were superior to their husbands as prophets.

Women were also highly respected. In the Ten Commandments, we are told to "Honor your father and your mother" in Ex. 20:12, but to "respect his mother and father" in Lev. 19:3. The fact that father comes first in one case, but mother in the other, was taken to mean that we are to honor both parents equally.

Although women's primary role was as the mother and keeper of the household, they were not limited to the domestic sphere. Women had the right to own, buy and sell property and to engage in business, following the example of Proverbs 31. They also had more rights with respect to marriage than in most other cultures, and under no circumstances could they be beaten or abused by their husbands.

To be sure, the Talmud says some negative things about women, with some rabbis describing them as being lazy, gluttonous, gossips, and prone to witchcraft; of course, they also describe men as being prone to lust and sexual sin. Overall, though, there can be no serious question that Jewish women were far more highly regarded and far better off than their pagan neighbors, stereotypes to the contrary notwithstanding.

CHRISTIANITY

Christianity carried on this tradition of honoring women. Women played important supporting roles in Jesus' ministry and were the first witnesses of the Resurrection. Spiritually, the distinction between men and women is erased in Christ (Gal. 3:28). Women converted to Christianity in large numbers, in part because of the respect and freedom it gave them. Some of these even became leaders in the early church, sponsoring churches in their homes (e.g. Col. 4:15) and serving as deacons[1] and prophets (e.g. Acts 21:9).

---

1   In addition to Phoebe (Rom. 16:1), the Roman writer Pliny the Younger wrote a letter to the Emperor Trajan asking him how to handle Christians and noting that he had arrested two female slaves who were deaconesses.

Women continued to play important roles in the church into the middle ages and beyond, including powerful and influential abbesses who ran women's convents and sometimes double monasteries (that is, two monasteries close together, one for men and one for women), founders of religious orders such as St. Claire, mystics and visionaries such as Hildegard von Bingen and Theresa of Avila, and in the modern world highly respected religious leaders such as Mother Theresa.

Christian ethical standards also raised the status of women. Husbands were commanded to love and take care of their wives as Christ loved and took care of the church (Eph. 5:25), an unheard of idea in the Greco-Roman world. The impact of Christianity on family life is important enough to deserve its own study, so we will return to that topic in the next chapter. For now, suffice it to say that here again, Christianity markedly improved the marital conditions for women compared to the pagan world.

Christians also joined the Jews in rejecting abortion and infanticide, but went further in rescuing abandoned babies—mostly girls—and raising them in their own households.

At the same time, it must be said that the Church has not always been true to its foundations in its treatment of women. A great deal of the problem here comes from the influence of Greek misogyny on early Christian writers, who imported negative ideas about women from Aristotle, from Neo-Platonists, and from other pagan sources. It certainly does not originate from the Biblical concept of men's and women's shared creation in the image of God, nor from Jewish theory or practice.

Despite stereotypes to the contrary, Judaism and Christianity have had a more positive impact on women than any other movement in history. The image of God in both male and female was the foundation for women's rights and the ultimate source for modern ideas of gender equality. Scripture affirms that though men and women are different, they are equally valuable before God, equally worthy of honor and respect, and spiritually and morally equal in Christ.

QUESTIONS

1. Read Proverbs 31. What does this passage tell you about Israelite ideals of the role of women in the family and society?

2. Where do you see women's rights and status under attack in the world today? In what ways do you see practices similar to those of the ancient world? What should be our response to these attacks?

3. Think about the views of women that are common in our culture today. In what ways do they correspond to the teachings of the Bible? In what ways do they depart from the Bible?

4. Why do you think it is important to understand the role of Judaism and Christianity in the development of women's rights throughout history?

5. Using what you now know, how would you respond to someone who claims that Christianity is oppressive to women?

6. How do you reconcile the Bible's affirmation of differences between the genders with the Bible's insistence that men and women are equal image bearers of God? How does this play out in families, churches and society as a whole?

The Image of God

F O U R

The Image of God and Marriage

Male and Female Together

As we have seen in the previous chapter, Genesis 1:27 states that the image of God is contained in both males and females equally. At the same time, however, given the overall context of the creation account in Genesis 1 and 2, we can take this one step further to see the image of God as not simply enshrined in us as individuals, but especially in the union of male and female together in marriage.

To understand why this is the case, we need to look at the story of the creation of Eve in Genesis 2 and its implications elsewhere in Scripture.

> *The LORD God said, "It is not good for the man to be alone. I will make a helper suitable for him."... So the LORD God caused the man to fall into a deep sleep; and while he was sleeping, he took one of the man's ribs and closed up the place with flesh. Then the LORD God made a woman from the rib he had taken out of the man, and he brought her to the man. The man said, "This is now bone of my bones and flesh of my flesh; she shall be called 'woman,' for she was taken out of man." For this reason a man will leave his father and mother and be united to his wife, and they will become one flesh. —Gen. 2:18, 21-24*

Commentators noticed early on the difference between this description of the creation of Eve and Genesis 1:27, which can be taken to mean that man and woman were created together. One suggested resolution comes from the *Midrash Rabbah*, which states that man was originally created as a hermaphrodite and then God separated the sexes. While we don't need to go that far to find an explanation for the differences in the two chapters, there is an important element of truth here: in a very real sense, the "man" as created in the image of God includes male and female together as a unit.

A PARTNERSHIP IN LOVE

Let's take a closer look at what's being said in Genesis 2. First, we should note that this is the only place in the creation accounts in which God pronounces something *not* good. It is not good for man to be alone, *because he was made to be a social being*. Animals were not adequate as his companions, so God created Eve from Adam's side (a better translation than "rib"). Eve was thus part of him and so could not be considered either inferior or a part of the creation over which Adam was to have dominion.

For all the misogyny that creeps into medieval theologians, many of the most important ones got it right on this point. To take just one example, Peter Lombard's *Sentences*, which was the basic textbook for theology in the Middle Ages, cites St. Augustine when he addressed the question of why God used one of Adam's ribs to make Eve:

> *Moreover from these causes "woman was made from man, not from any part of the man's body, but she was formed from his side, so that there might be shown, that she was created in a partnership of love, lest perchance, if she had been made from [his] head, she might seem to be preferred to man for [his] domination, or if from [his] feet, to be subjected [to him] for [his] service. Therefore because for man there was*

prepared neither a lady nor a handmade, but a com-
panion, she was to be produced neither from [his]
head nor from [his] feet, but from [his] side, so that
she might recognize that she [was] to be placed along-
side him, she whom he had learned to recognize as the
one taken from his side."[1]

These comments, of course, reinforce the point that since the image of God is shared between men and women, they are intrinsically equal before God; they also explain why it is totally inappropriate and unbiblical for husbands to be domineering over their wives. But Lombard and Augustine also point ahead toward Adam's reaction to the creation of Eve. In Genesis 2:23, Adam recognizes Eve as part of himself, and so names her *Woman* (Hebrew *ishshah*) because she was taken out of *Man* (Hebrew *ish*). Since in Hebrew thought, a being's name was supposed to reflect its nature, the derivation of the word for woman indicates the deep, intimate connection between woman and man.

Woman's origin from Man, leads directly to the next verse: Man is to leave his parents and be joined to Woman—in other words, he is to marry and form a new family unit. And this is accomplished by the two "becoming one flesh" through sexual relations, in essence providing wholeness by reuniting Adam with his Rib.

So the image of God in Genesis 1:27 is encompassed equally by men and women, but most fully by man and woman together, as a family. The family is the fundamental unit within society, and is thus the place at which human dominion/stewardship over the world is first exercised.

SCRIPTURE ON MARRIAGE

There are several points that follow from the nature of marriage in Scripture. The first, as Jesus affirmed, is that marriage

---

1   *Sentences*, book 2, distinction 18, question 2; see http://www.francis-can-archive.org/lombardus/opera/ ls2-18.html, citing Augustine, *On the Literal Meaning of Genesis* 9.13.23. See also Thomas Aquinas, *Summa Theologica* 1, q. 92, 3, http://www.newadvent.org/sum ma/1092.htm#article3.

is meant to be permanent: God joins men and women together into one flesh, and so we should not try to undo what God has done (Mk. 10:2-9). Even from an anthropological perspective this makes sense: all cultures have marriage as a privileged institution, even though it might take a variety of forms, because creates a stable environment to bring children into the world and to provide for them. Allowing marriages to dissolve easily disrupts its role in child-rearing. And for Christians, our understanding of the unity of the two into one flesh should make us do everything we can to insure the permanence of marriage.

Second, the deep, intimate unity within marriage points to the depth of the Church's relationship and unity with Jesus. In the Old Testament, God often describes Israel as His wife, particularly by identifying idolatry with adultery (e.g. Hos. 1:2). In the New Testament, the Church is described as the Body of Christ, and He is united with it in the same way that husbands and wives are one flesh (Eph. 6:31-32). The love that is to characterize marriage, the intimate fellowship, and the unity we are to experience are a picture to the Apostle Paul of our relationship with Christ. These ideas led the Church early on to move away from the polygamy practiced in the pagan world and to some extent in ancient Israel and to insist on monogamy as the proper form for marriage: one man, one woman, one lifetime.

The Church's teaching on the permanence of marriage and its emphasis on monogamy had an enormous effect on improving women's place in society. No longer could a woman be divorced because she had no sons or was past childbearing age. No longer could wealthy men take multiple wives, diminishing their role in the household and depriving poorer men of spouses. As Vishal Mangalwadi points out, monogamy in particular led to social structures in the West that had a tremendously positive effect on society, so much so that in India even Hindus pushed to mandate monogamy as an essential prerequisite for modernization.[2] Given

---

2   *Must the Sun Set on the West,* audio CD series, *From Luther's Vicarage to Hefner's Harem: Turning Men into (Play)boys and Women into "Desperate Housewives."*

that this is God's design for humanity, it should come as no surprise that it produces better results than the alternatives.

Third, marriage is a reflection of the Trinity. The doctrine of the Trinity says that the three Persons of the Godhead are all one, yet in some sense distinct from each other. Just as a cube with a width of one meter, a height of one meter, and a depth of one meter, has a volume of one cubic meter, so the three persons of the Trinity complement each other, each participating in all the attributes of deity, but the Godhead is only fully defined by the interrelationships of the three together. The significance of this is that God is an intrinsically relational being in and of Himself, living in eternal loving relations between Father, Son and Spirit. Thus humanity made in His image is, as we have seen, relational. And man and woman as the two equals becoming one flesh in marriage provides us with a two dimensional picture of our three dimensional God.

FOUNDATION FOR SEXUAL ETHICS

Lastly, Genesis 2:24 is the foundation for sexual ethics. Sexual activity is designed to unite a man and a woman together in a permanent bond. Even our biology points to this, as the hormonal response to sexual activity increases emotional attachment to your partner. This is one reason why sexual activity is restricted to marriage—the potential to cause devastating emotional damage to ourselves and each other is so great, it requires the protection of a permanent, committed, loving relationship. Our society's experience today with "sexual liberation" demonstrates the wisdom of the Biblical view. Although it is rarely seen in this light, marriage is the place where the full image of God found in male and female together is best seen and expressed. This is all the more reason for us to work to restore our commitment to and advocacy for a Biblical vision of sexuality and marriage in our churches and society.

Questions

1. Why was it "not good" for the man to be alone in Genesis? Explain why this "not good" condition reflects the image of God.

2. There is a great deal of confusion about the nature of marriage today. How does society view the nature and purpose of marriage today? Read Matt. 19:3-9. What was Jesus' understanding of marriage? How does it compare to the views of our culture?

3. Sexual activity is a driving force in American culture and politics, as evidenced by media, regulatory policy concerning healthcare, court decisions, and political platforms. What do Jesus' words in the above passage suggest about our culture's freewheeling attitudes toward sex? Read 1 Cor. 6:12-20. What does this passage add to Jesus' teaching about sexual activity?

4. Read Eph. 5:21-33. Describe the responsibilities of husbands and wives in this passage. How does vs. 21 affect the way you interpret the passage? How does this passage fit with the argument in the chapter that biblical marriage and monogamy are good for women?

5. What does Eph. 5:21-33 tell us about the work of Christ and His relationship to the church? What does Christ's work tell us about the nature of marriage?

6. What can Christians today do to help recover a biblical understanding of the marriage in the church and in society?

F I V E

THE IMAGE OF GOD AND SPIRITUALITY

IN GOD'S IMAGE

In the first articles of this series, we observed that the image of God means that we are created to be God's representatives, regents, and stewards on earth; that this position is the foundation for human dignity and rights; that it applies equally to men and women; and that it is expressed most directly in the family, as the fundamental unit in society and therefore the place where our dominion over creation is first exercised.

The tools God has given humanity to carry out this work of stewardship—creativity, reason, the ability to make choices, the will, emotions, morality—all of these share one important characteristic: they are all expressions of the non-physical side of human nature – that is, the fact that in addition to having physical bodies, we are spiritual beings as well.[1]

CHALLENGES TO SPIRITUALITY

Contemporary culture poses several challenges to the Biblical idea of spirituality. First, one common worldview, known as

---

1   Scripture divides humans up in a variety of ways: body, soul and spirit; body and soul; heart, soul, mind and strength; etc. For our purposes here, we are not looking at a precise distinction between the different aspects of human nature, but simply using "spirit" to describe all of humanity's non-physical traits.

materialism or *naturalism*, says that the physical world of matter and energy is all that exists, and thus that people have no non-physical side. This view is most common within the scientific community, particularly among those who believe that the natural sciences provide the only reliable approach to knowledge about any and everything, an idea known as scientism.

To believe this, however, runs counter to our own experience of life. First, it argues that our consciousness is nothing more than a result of chemistry in our brains; free will is an illusion, since everything we do is the result of physics and chemistry; love, hate, self-consciousness, our awareness of ourselves, all are just chemical reactions. Good and evil and right and wrong do not exist since they are neither matter nor energy; you cannot even call them cultural preferences since a preference is neither matter nor energy either.

In fact, even the thoughts you are having right now as you read this aren't thoughts in the way you think they are— they're just neurons firing as a result of electrical impulses from your optic nerves. And if you want to argue with these conclusions, you can no more help yourself from doing that or from holding your views than the moon can stop orbiting the earth. You are nothing more than a robot carrying out the necessary and inevitable results of physics, chemistry, and biology.

While some people argue this, it is extremely doubtful that they really believe it deep down. And it is certain that they do not and cannot live as if it were true.

A second problem revolves around the word "spiritual" itself. People frequently describe themselves as "spiritual, but not religious" or talk about someone being "very spiritual." The problem is, if you ask what they mean by the word, "spiritual," they typically cannot define it. It seems to mean something like an interest in metaphysical issues, habitual living in the moment, or a sense of connection to some kind of non-physical "higher being" or "beings."

Even though a "spiritual" person's spiritual practices (i.e. exercises done to get in touch with the higher beings or to attain metaphysical experiences or knowledge) may be done as part of a group, spirituality is rarely seen in corporate terms—it tends to be highly individual, which is in part what separates it in people's minds from religion. This emphasis on intuition and experience makes it very close to the ancient heresy of *Gnosticism*, which believed that salvation is attained through acquiring secret knowledge (or discovering it within you).

While this idea of spirituality has some positive elements, particularly its recognition of the existence of the non-physical dimensions of reality, it rarely reflects the Biblical concept of what it means that human beings are spiritual creatures. It often leans toward a form of *dualism*, another element of ancient Gnosticism. Gnostics believed that the spiritual world was far superior to the physical world, so much so that the physical is irrelevant at best or completely evil at worst. This idea shows up in Christian Science, in many Eastern religions and New Age teachings, and ironically in some forms of Christian fundamentalism.

Yet Scripture tells us that God pronounced the physical world that He created very good—including our bodies. In fact, our bodies are essential for us to carry out our mandate to be God's stewards over the physical world: we have to be *in* it to take care *of* it. How, then, can the body be evil?

Even humanity's fall into sin doesn't change the essential goodness of the body, especially since sin comes from our inner, non-physical being, not our bodies (Mark 7:14-23).[2] We will return to the effects of Fall in chapter 11.

AN INTEGRATED WHOLE

Instead of dividing body and spirit, the Bible teaches that the human being is an integrated whole, simultaneously physical

---

2   Paul's use of the term "flesh" as the opposite of "spirit" (e.g. Rom. 8:5) does not refer to the physical body. In context, it refers to an attitude of rebellion against the Holy Spirit's leading of our lives in obedience to God.

and spiritual, with both created good. This unity is reflected in the word for "spirit" in both Hebrew (*ruah*) and Greek (*pneuma*), which refers not just to spirit, but to breath. While it is possible to take this too far, the connection of spirit and breath points to the fact that it is the union of spirit and body that gives us life (e.g. Gen. 2:7).

To put it differently, we cannot separate our understanding of what it means for us to be spiritual creatures from our bodies. Neither the *materialist* who ignores the reality of the spirit, nor the *Gnostic* who rejects the significance of the body, are correct. The spirit and the body are united in us, and must be understood together.

Of course, even animals have "the breath of life" (Gen. 7:21-22). The human spirit goes well beyond simply giving us biological life. As medieval theologians and Renaissance thinkers pointed out, humanity is unique as a microcosm of the creation: we are both physical and spiritual creatures; we are both sensual and rational; we participate in both time and eternity. What creature is thus in a better position to act as God's regent (or, in ancient near eastern terms, His image) on earth?

BIBLICAL SPIRITUALITY

So what is the Biblical concept of spirituality? Jesus tells us that "God is spirit, and those who worship Him must worship in spirit and truth." (Jn. 4:24) Our ability to worship God, to connect with Him, even to have a personal relationship with Him, hinges on the fact that we have within us a spirit that is in some measure a reflection, an image, of God's Spirit. Without the ability of our spirit to connect with God as spirit, worship cannot happen.

This is the nature of true spirituality: worshipping God who is Spirit. Even this, however, cannot be separated from our bodies. Rom. 12:1 tells us that true worship occurs as we present our bodies as living sacrifices to God. The Greek word translated as "body" is *soma*, which points to the person as an integrated whole – bodies, minds, emotions and will.

This echoes Jesus' restatement of the *shema*, the foundation of Judaism, which tells us that we are to love God with all our heart, soul, mind and strength—the whole being (Mark 12:29).[3]

All we think, say, and do is thus to be done for the love of God, as part of presenting our whole selves as living sacrifices to Him, which is true worship and true spirituality. This is another way of expressing our calling as God's stewards on earth: all that we do here, we are to do in His name, for His sake, to express our love for Him and to glorify Him.

---

3   One implication of this is that taking proper care of our bodies is an aspect of true spirituality. While we do not worship the body, we must take care of it and develop it just as we do our minds and our "spiritual life" as part of our stewardship of ourselves before God.

QUESTIONS

1. Of the two extremes of materialism and Gnosticism, which have you run into the most? Describe some specific examples that you have encountered. Do you see either present in the church?

2. How would you define the words "spiritual" and "spirituality?" How do people grow spiritually?

3. Read John 4:1-26. What does Jesus identify as the critical requirements for true worship? Why do you think He lists these rather than anything else?

4. Read Mark 12:28-31. What can you do to grow in loving God with your heart? With your soul? With your mind? With your strength? What is the relationship between loving God and spirituality?

5. Read Rom. 12:1-2. What is the role of the body in our "spiritual service" (Greek: *latreia*, service or worship to God)? Have you ever considered the role of the body in worship? Does developing the body have a place in our spirituality? In loving God? Why or why not?

6. What is the danger we face in Rom. 12:2? Do you see this problem in the church today? How do we avoid this trap, and conversely, how are we transformed? Why do you think the mind (Greek *nous*, the part of the mind that understands what is true and real; intuition; imagination; common sense) is so important to Paul?

7. Do you see spirituality as individual, corporate, or both? How do your spiritual life and activities reflect your answer?

S I X

THE IMAGE OF GOD AND CREATIVITY

IN GOD'S IMAGE

Although the term "image of a god" in the ancient near east conveyed the idea of being a representative or steward of a god, the Biblical phrase also points to those things in human beings that make us similar to God and thus enable us to carry out our charge as His regents in the world. In this and the next several chapters, we will explore aspects of our nature that reflect God's own attributes, and look at some of their implications for our work as God's stewards. We begin with creativity.

CREATIVITY AND HUMAN LIFE

Christians don't talk much about creativity as a crucial aspect of what it means to be human, and few formal theologians address it in connection with the image of God. Part of the reason for this is history: originally, theologians argued that only God could "create" (Latin *creare*), which for them meant producing something out of nothing (Latin *ex nihilo*); human beings could only "make" (Latin *facere*) things out of already existing material.

And yet, as Dorothy Sayers pointed out, "It is observable that in the passage leading up to the statement ... [that man is made in the image of God], he has given no detailed information about God. Looking at man, he sees in him something essentially divine, but when we turn back to see what he says about the original upon which the 'image' of God was modelled, we find only the single assertion, 'God created'. The characteristic common to God and man is apparently that: the desire and the ability to make things."[1]

Similarly, J.R.R. Tolkien, another great English writer who travelled in the same circles as Sayers, emphasized the idea of "sub-creation" in producing his fantasy works, striving to create a coherent, consistent secondary world. He saw this process of sub-creation "as a form of worship, a way for creatures to express the divine image in them by becoming creators."[2]

So what exactly is creativity? The term is curiously difficult to define, though obviously it has something to do with the ability to create—"the desire and the ability to make things," as Sayers put it. Not surprisingly, the early chapters of Genesis and the mandate to "have dominion" over the world outline some of the big picture elements of creativity.

IN THE BEGINNING

God gave Adam two jobs in Eden. First, Adam was "to work and keep" the Garden (Gen. 2:15). The Garden is specifically described not just as a place where food grew, but as a place of beauty and delight (Gen. 2:9); we may thus infer that working and keeping the Garden involved not simply food production, but cultivating beauty as well. In other words, the arts have been

---

1   *The Mind of the Maker*, http://www.worldinvisible.com/library/dlsayers/mindofmaker/mind.02.htm. This book is the most thorough treatment of creativity as central to what it means to be human and to the image of God that I have seen. It is no accident that Sayers was a novelist, playwright, poet and translator—in other words, a person engaged in "creative writing"—rather than a formal theologian.

2   David C. Downing, "Sub-Creation or Smuggled Theology: Tolkien contra Lewis on Christian Fantasy," http://www.cslewisinstitute.org/cslewis/downing_theology.htm. This idea is also reflected in the story, "Of Aulë and Yavanna," chapter 2 of *The Silmarillion*.

part of God's mandate to humanity from the very beginning. There can be no question that God loves beauty. Consider the earth and stars as celebrated in the Psalms, or the specifications of the Tabernacle and its furnishings, as well as the priests' garments, in Ex. 26-28 and 30, or the Temple in 1 Kg. 6-7, or the throne room of Heaven in Is. 6 and Rev. 4, or the New Jerusalem in Rev. 21. Both God's works and His worship are bathed in beauty.

Even more remarkably, God told Moses, "See, I have called by name Bezalel, the son of Uri, the son of Hur, of the tribe of Judah. *I have filled him with the Spirit of God* in wisdom, in understanding, in knowledge, and in all kinds of craftsmanship, to make artistic designs for work in gold, in silver, and in bronze, and in the cutting of stones for settings, and in the carving of wood, that he may work in all kinds of craftsmanship. And behold, I Myself have appointed with him Oholiab, the son of Ahisamach, of the tribe of Dan ; and in the hearts of all who are skillful I have put skill, that they may make all that I have commanded you...." (Ex. 31:2-6, emphasis added) So the craftsmanship and skill that went into the making the Tabernacle, as well as the ability "to make artistic designs," were the products of being filled with the Holy Spirit, and therefore reflect something of God's own nature.

The artist, in using the materials God has placed at hand and the skills which God has given, is thus a sub-creator, to use Tolkien's word, exercising the image of God by fulfilling the mandate to work and keep the Garden.

Adam's second task was naming the animals (Gen. 2:19-20). This also was a creative act, though of a different type. In Hebrew, a being's name was thought to reflect its nature, and thus to name the animals appropriately required studying and understanding them, and then coming up with the appropriate word to encapsulate their nature. We will return to this in chapter 9 when we consider the sciences. For now, we need to note that the act of naming is **an** intellectual and creative activity, and as a result a full biblical understanding of human creativity includes not just the visual arts but the verbal arts as well.[3]

Language is, of course, a characteristic of God Himself. He spoke the universe into existence, and Jesus is described in John 1 as the word of God. Our use of language is thus another reflection of the image of God, particularly when we use words to create.

CREATIVITY IN LANGUAGE

The nature of Scripture itself affirms the importance of creativity in language. God did not reveal Himself through a list of essential doctrines or a schematic outline of theology. Instead, He chose to reveal Himself through the writings of a variety of authors over many hundreds of years in just about every type of literature then known to humanity. There are historical narratives, laws, poems and songs, proverbs, prophetic oracles, parables, letters, apocalyptic literature, even genealogies. In producing our own literature, we are following the example of God who gave us a rich literary heritage in His word.

This is precisely the kind of creativity both Dorothy Sayers and J.R.R. Tolkien had in mind when they talked about "making things" or "sub-creation," though of course they would not have limited creative activity to literature. At the same time, however, both saw writing as a very high level creative act since it involves bringing imagination to life using words just as God Himself did at the Creation. Of course, God's words produced physical results, whereas the main fruit of writing is not the physical book but the ideas it conveys.

CREATIVITY IN MUSIC

Another area of creative activity found in Scripture is music. God is surrounded by music in Heaven (Is. 6; Rev. 4, 5, 11, 15,

---

3   There is common ground between visual and verbal arts. Bezalel had intelligence and knowledge, which empowered his craftsmanship; Adam needed the same qualities in naming animals, though he applied them using a different vehicle than the physical objects Bezazel produced. It thus seems fair to say that some type of intellectual ability is a prerequisite for creative work.

etc.). God's actions in history were celebrated in song (e.g. Ex. 15:1-21), and music was central to the worship in Jerusalem (e.g. 1 Chron. 15:16-24). Jesus and the Apostles sang hymns (Matt. 26:30), as did Paul and Silas even when they were locked in the deepest part of a Roman prison (Acts 16:25).

Psalms, the longest book in the Bible, is a collection of songs, and it celebrates not only singing but instrumental music (e.g. Ps. 150) as a means of praising God. The Psalms include songs of praise, laments, pleas for help, introspection, prayers of repentance .... In any and every circumstance, it gives us examples of how to sing our heart's cries to God.

The Apostle Paul even tells us that music is a sign of being filled with the Spirit (Eph. 5:18-20). Singing thus joins Bezalel's visual arts as a work of the Holy Spirit and therefore as an aspect of the image of God.

CREATIVITY IN ALL OF LIFE

Creativity extends well beyond just these few examples here. In every area of life, at our home, in our work, and in our recreation, creativity plays a major role. The reason is simple: part of our nature as image bearers of God the Creator is to be sub-creators, and so to carry out our original mandate which God gave us in the Garden, to create culture as a function of our stewardship of the world.

QUESTIONS

1. How would you define creativity? Would you agree with J.R.R. Tolkien that creative activity is a form of worship? Why or why not?

2. Describe the jobs that God gave to Adam in the Garden. Why is creativity essential to carrying them out?

3. Read Ex. 31:2-6. Describe the results of being filled with the Spirit in Bezalel's life. What does this suggest about the nature of spiritual gifts? Have you ever considered the possibility that you are specifically gifted by God to carry out your job?

4. Historically, the church has been a major patron of both visual and musical arts, and Christianity has been an inspiration for great literature and drama. Was this an appropriate use of resources? Why or why not? Do you think that the church and individual Christians are sufficiently involved in sponsoring great art today?

5. Read Ps. 150. List the ways we are told to praise God. How many of these do you incorporate into your personal life? How many are used in your church? Do you think we should use more of these today? Why or why not?

6. In addition to the arts, what other fields require creativity? In what ways do those fields reflect the image of God as discussed in the first chapters of this book?

7. When engaged in a creative endeavor, have you ever felt inspired or empowered by something beyond yourself? If so, do you think this was the work of the Spirit, or just your imagination? Explain your answer.

S E V E N

THE IMAGE OF GOD AND REASON

GOD AND REASON

Of all the creatures in the physical world, only human beings share with God the ability to reason. It is not surprising, then, that when theologians discuss aspects of the image of God, reason almost always tops the list. From the perspective of our calling as stewards of the world, reason is one of the most important tools we have been given. So as we explore the implications of our creation in God's image, we must take a closer look at human rationality. Before we do that, however, we should first back up a step and look at reason as an attribute of God.

Scripture over and over again recognizes that God is rational. We see this first in God's work of creation. In Genesis, we are told that God looked at what He has made and evaluated it as "good" (Gen. 1:10, 12, etc.), "not good" (Gen. 2:18), or "very good" (Gen. 1:31). This evaluation necessarily involved a rational judgment about the creation. The Scriptures frequently extol God's wisdom, which can be defined as the practical application of divine knowledge. Proverbs tells us that God created the world through wisdom (e.g. Prov. 3:19-20), and the Psalms celebrate God's wisdom displayed in creation (e.g. Ps. 104:24).

The supreme example in Scripture of God's rationality is found in John 1:1-3: "In the beginning was the Word (Gk. *logos*), and the Word was with God and the Word was God. He was in the beginning with God. All things were made through Him, and without him was not anything made that was made."

Logos, the Greek word translated here as "Word," is a far richer term than "word" is in English. In Platonic thought, the *logos* was the creative principle through which the world came into existence. In Stoicism, it was the rational principle which governed the universe. In common use, it is the root word for "logic," and pointed to both knowledge and thought.

So Christ as the *Logos* of God is the sum total of all that can be known (cf. Col. 2:3), the ultimate example of divine reason and wisdom (1 Cor. 1:24).

REASONING WITH US

Not surprisingly, then, God sometimes appeals to reason to try to get through to us. For example, in Is. 44:9-20, God offers a devastating critique of idolatry, appealing to common sense to show how foolish it is. And in Is. 1:18-20, He invites Judah to reason with Him: repentance and obedience produces forgiveness and blessing; rebellion brings destruction; which course makes more sense?

Of course, God's rationality is far beyond our own. In Is. 55:8-9, God tells us, "... My thoughts are not your thoughts, Nor are your ways My ways," declares the LORD. "For as the heavens are higher than the earth, So are My ways higher than your ways And My thoughts than your thoughts." So human reason can only take us so far when it comes to knowing and understanding God and why He governs the world as He does. For that, we need revelation, which comes to us both through the natural world and Scripture. This is why Prov. 3:5 exhorts us to "Trust in the LORD with all your heart, and do not lean on your own understanding." Reason has is limits, especially when it comes to understanding God and His ways.

WHAT IS REASON?

So God is rational—super-rational, but rational nonetheless. What does God's rationality tell us about human reason? And what exactly is reason?

As is frequently the case with terms like this, reason is not easy to define simply. On a human level, reason is the ability to reach conclusions based on premises. The premises can be abstract ideas, such as the ones used in mathematics, or they can be based on personal experience and observation, such as "if you put your hand in a fire, you will get burned," or some combination of the two, as is frequently the case in the sciences. [1]

Although a fairly simple concept, reason is a deceptively powerful tool which we use constantly in exercising our mandate to be stewards of the world. Reason enables us to do everything from figuring out cause and effect, to learning that planting seeds leads to growing plants, to understanding the importance of water in the natural world, to figuring out irrigation systems, to learning what works and what doesn't in putting up buildings, to developing mathematics and then applying it to real world situations, and more. The same ability that led our ancient ancestors to fashion stone tools enabled us to develop iPads and space probes. They all come from reason based on observation, experience, and sometimes abstract premises.

THE IMPORTANCE OF REASON

Reason is thus critically important for our work with the physical world: without it, we cannot exercise our proper dominion under God. But reason extends beyond just under-

---

1   Scientific theories are supposed to be supported by observations though in practice particularly powerful theories become paradigms through which all subsequent observations and evidence are interpreted. At that point the governing theory becomes a form of abstract premise. The reigning paradigms in science are considered foundational and for all practical purposes certain, until enough counter-evidence develops, leading to the emergence of a new theory which overturns the old paradigm.

standing the laws of nature. For example, we can engage in moral reasoning, thinking through the ethical implications of actions, ideas and policies based on principles of right and wrong. We can use reason to try to understand the people around us—what motivates them, why they do or say the things they do, etc. And through both principles and experience, we can learn how to interact effectively with others. In all of these cases, reason is an effective tool because it deals with our experiences as physical creatures. We interact with the natural world and with other people on a daily basis, and so we can study, experiment, observe, and think through our experiences. This is even true of ethical issues, since they too deal with life in this world. Things get more complex, however, when it comes to spiritual matters.

Many philosophers argue that spirituality is a matter of faith, and faith is completely divorced from reason. They reject any connection between reason and "authority," mystical experience, intuition or faith. There is an element of truth in this: if you follow a New Age teacher's techniques and enter an altered state of consciousness, it does not logically follow that the teacher's explanation of that experience is automatically correct. Neither the authority of the teacher nor the experience itself provides enough to evaluate what happened rationally.

At the same time, however, the argument against authority and faith is clearly overdrawn. For example, in practice those who make this argument against authority frequently themselves rely on authority. How many of them can prove that the Earth goes around the Sun, as opposed to accepting it as true because of the authority of scientists? If they can prove it, do they do so relying on their own observations, or are they accepting someone else's as authoritative? Or how many of them rely on experts (authorities) for medical care, or any of the thousands of other areas of life where we look to experts to explain things for us?

Beyond this inconsistency, however, lies the underlying

problem that all reason is ultimately based on unproven assumptions that must be taken on faith. We cannot prove that our observations are accurate, that our minds are capable of understanding the world, that cause and effect are really linked, that other minds exist. All knowledge is ultimately based on faith—on accepting unproven and unprovable assumptions as true.

To argue that faith and reason are separate, incompatible spheres is thus simply false. Reason relies on faith as its starting point.

As a result, despite the fact that God is infinite and we are not, we can even reason about Him. In fact, Christianity more or less demands the development of theology, which Rodney Stark defines as "formal reasoning about God."[2] As Stark points out, "...unlike Muhammad or Moses, whose texts were accepted as divine transmissions and therefore have encouraged literalism, Jesus wrote nothing, and from the very start the church fathers were forced to reason as to the implications of a collection of his remembered sayings—the New Testament is not a unified scripture but an *anthology*. Consequently, the precedent for deduction and inference and for the idea of theological progress began with Paul: 'For our knowledge is imperfect and our prophecy is imperfect.'"[3]

Christianity thus requires the use of human reason to draw a coherent picture of God and His dealings with humanity from the biblical texts. This study of the texts leads to greater and greater insight into the Bible as each generation builds on the work of previous scholars. And according to Stark, this idea of theological progress led to a more general idea of intellectual progress, ultimately resulting in the use of reason in science, economics, and politics, creating much of the modern Western world.[4]

---

2   *The Victory of Reason*, 5.

3   Ibid., 9.

4   Ibid., 12.

Far from being in opposition, reason and faith are thus deeply intertwined with each other. Both are necessary and important tools that God has given us to understand the world, each other, and Him, and to fulfill our purpose as His stewards in the world.

QUESTIONS

1. Read Prov. 3:19-20 and Ps. 104, noting particularly vs. 24. How is God's wisdom displayed in the creation? When you look at the world, do you see evidence of a rational mind behind it, or simply time and random chance?

2. Read John 1:1-3; 1 Cor. 1:20-25; Col. 2:1-4. What do these verses tell us about Jesus and His relationship with God's rationality? How does this expand your understanding of who Jesus is?

3. What role does reason play in our relationships with other people? Is it more authentic to act on the basis of our emotions than reason as we deal with people? Why or why not? Similarly, what place does reason play in ethical and moral decision-making?

4. The chapter argues that faith and reason are intertwined— that you cannot have reason without faith, and that faith is supported by reason. Do you agree or disagree? Why?

5. Read Eph. 1:17-19, 3:16-19; Phil. 1:9-11; Col. 1:9-12. Notice how often Paul uses words like knowledge, wisdom, discernment, and understanding. Why do you think Paul puts so much emphasis on this in his prayers for these churches?

6. What is the role of reason in our spiritual life? Is it a help or a hindrance? What is the right balance between theology, mystery, and practice?

THE IMAGE OF GOD

E I G H T

THE IMAGE OF GOD AND WORK

WHY WE WORK

In the last two chapters, we looked at creativity and reason as two aspects of the image of God that are essential tools for carrying out our mandate to create culture and to act as His stewards in this world. Before considering other aspects of human nature that reflect God's image, this chapter and the next will look at ways that creativity and reason work together in fulfilling the work God gave us in Eden. We begin with a closer look at the command to tend the Garden.

In our culture, work is often seen as something we do only because we have to. In contrast, the biblical attitude is that work is something we do because of who we are. Work is the fulfillment of our nature as beings made in God's image. Gen. 2:2 tells us that God worked when He created the world, or His Sabbath rest would be meaningless, and so His command to Adam to tend the Garden reflects His own nature as one who works.

This same idea is seen in the fourth commandment. As Del Tackett points out in *The Truth Project*, we think of this as the Sabbath commandment, but it might be better to think of it as the labor commandment:

> *Six days you shall labor and do all your work, but the seventh day is a Sabbath to the LORD your God. On*

*it you shall not do any work, neither you, nor your son
or daughter, nor your manservant or maidservant, nor
your animals, nor the alien within your gates. For in six
days the LORD made the heavens and the earth, the sea,
and all that is in them, but he rested on the seventh day.
Therefore the LORD blessed the Sabbath day and made
it holy. —Ex. 20:9-11*

We take the Sabbath off because God did, but we also
work the other six days because God did. The fact is, work
can be very fulfilling and important for us; it can also become
addictive or be used as an excuse to avoid something else that
needs our attention. As a result, God had to tell us to take
time off.

There is another important respect in which our work is
related to God's: Adam's responsibility to tend the Garden
was actually a command to continue and complete the work
that God had begun. Our labor, using the resources He has
placed in our hands, is an act of sub-creation that is intended
to bring out the potential He has placed in the world.

WORK AND CULTURE

This can be seen in the overall trajectory of biblical history.
Creation begins formless and void, and God puts it in order.
When He places Adam in the Garden, He doesn't intend for
Adam to simply stay there. It is no accident that the Bible begins in a garden but ends in a city. God's ultimate goal is not
to return us to some sort of pristine state of nature. Rather,
we are to develop culture (a word which comes from the Latin
cultus, meaning labor or cultivation), and ultimately to build
civilization, which comes from the Latin *civitas*, meaning city.

Put simply, the command to care for and tend the Garden does not mean merely to conserve what is there, but to
develop it responsibly as stewards of God's world toward the
advancement of civilization and culture. The principle is artic-
ulated forcefully in Jesus' parable of the talents (Matt. 25:14-
30): the only servant who is punished is the one who simply

conserved what he was given and did not try to use it to bring profit to the master. Why should our stewardship of the world be any different?

What this means is that our work to develop culture and civilization is a sacred act to a Christian, to be carried out as part of our mandate as the image of God in this world. All professions that are not inherently sinful can be God-given vocations, callings on our life, to carry out God's purposes in and for the world. We need to escape from the idea that some jobs are sacred and others merely secular: all work is and should be sacred to the Christian, done in full recognition that what we do in this world matters and can be done for the glory of God. This idea, known as the Cultural Mandate, is critical for understanding our role as God's stewards and for fulfilling Jesus' call to us to be salt and light in the world (Matt. 5:13-16, cf. Matt. 13:33).

The goodness and dignity of work also means that we should apply our reason to the task, so that as good stewards we make the best and most effective and efficient use of the resources available to us. We must always remember that the Earth is the Lord's, not ours, and though we need to develop its resources, we need to do so with care. Our reason and ingenuity are thus to be used in the task of responsibly creating culture and making the best possible long term use of what we have been given.

THE ECONOMIC SIGNIFICANCE OF WORK

So our work is important for advancing God's purposes in the world, and is an essential part of what it means to be human. But it also has economic significance. Genesis tells us that the Garden was both a source of food and a place of visual delight (Gen. 2:9). Adam was told to take care of the Garden and to eat the fruit that grew on the trees (Gen. 2:15-16). This is the very beginning of economics: as we tend the Garden, whether for the cultivation of beauty or the production of food, we are to earn our livelihood from our work.

The connection between the call to work and the provision of food points to one of the most basic of our God-given rights: the right to enjoy the fruits of our labor. This concept made its way into our culture in the traditional norm that people should be given an honest day's pay for an honest day's work. It has also been used to support the idea of workers' ownership of the means of production, collectivization, and Christian-influenced versions of communism. These and related ideas, however, do not do justice to the full biblical vision of labor, ownership, and rewards.

The right to the fruits of our labor leads directly to the idea of a right to property—in fact, it is hard to have the former without the latter. The Old Testament law presupposes a right to property, or the commandment against theft and the many property laws laid out in the Torah would make no sense at all.

This can be seen in the provisions for land ownership in Israel. A family's allotment of land was sacrosanct, so much so that when hard times hit, it could only be leased out, never sold. This meant that even the destitute in Israel would never be without hope of a fresh start for the family because their land could never be taken away from them forever. The right to property was absolute. This law also points to the idea that property rights extend to heirs, and thus that property can be inherited.

How seriously God took this law can be seen in the life of Ahab, arguably the worst king in Israel's history. He sponsored Baal worship and idolatry, and persecuted those trying to remain faithful to God, even murdering prophets (1 Kings 18:4). For these things he was roundly condemned by Elijah and other prophets throughout his reign. Significantly, however, the final, most severe judgment against him came after his wife arranged for Naboth to be framed for blasphemy and executed so that Ahab could claim his vineyard (1 Kings 21:1-26).[1] God had already pronounced a death sentence against

---

1 Since he was not directly responsible for Naboth's death and humbled himself before God, God held off the judgment until the days of his son (1 Kings 21:27-28).

Ahab for disobeying his express commands (1 Kings 20:42), but the judgment for the crimes against Naboth and his property led to an even more severe and horrifying judgment against Ahab and everyone in his entire household. Ahab had taken not only Naboth's life, but his family's place in Israel, so Ahab's family would itself be completely cut off from Israel. Significantly, it wasn't simply Naboth's murder that led to this judgment on Ahab's line. He was, after all, already guilty of multiple murders. The thing that set this apart was the crime against Naboth's property rights in Israel.

The right to property continues in the New Testament. The consistent testimony of the Scriptures points in this direction, from the commands against theft to the examples of Peter's continued ownership of his fishing boat (Jn. 21:3) or the wealthy Christians who opened their homes to the church. The one potential counter-example is Acts 2:44, which says that the believers in Jerusalem "had all things in common." Many people argue that this means that the church operated as a community of goods without any private property. But a careful reading of the text shows that this was not the case. The very next verse explains how "having all things in common" worked out in practice: people sold their possessions (not "all" their possessions, or they would then have themselves become among the destitute) to provide for those in need. In other words, they maintained ownership of their property until there was a need.

The church continued to recognize property ownership, as is clear from Peter's statements to Ananias in Acts 5:4, which treats the idea that Ananias had full rights to his property as obvious and beyond question. So even in a church that "had all things in common," property rights were seen as inviolable. In other words, people owned their own property but held it lightly, so that they freely parted with it to meet the needs of the poor in their community. Thus they simultaneously "had all things in common" and maintained private property.

A POSITIVE VISION OF WORK

Jews and Christians in the ancient world were unique in their perspective on the goodness and dignity of work, which other cultures saw only as drudgery fit for slaves and inferiors. At the same time, the recognition of property as an unalienable right, a right that preceded human government and thus as something that no king or government could arbitrarily revoke, created a stable environment for economic growth. We owe the positive vision of work, the incentives to be productive, and the security from arbitrary confiscation of our property—the hallmarks of traditional Western ideas of economics—to the long term impact of the biblical worldview on society.

QUESTIONS

1. What is your attitude toward work? Is it a necessary evil or something more? By some studies 95% of younger workers are regularly looking to change jobs. What does that suggest about the state of work in America today?

2. Read Ecclesiastes 2:4-11, 18-23; Luke 12:16-22. When does work become a danger to us? Have you ever met someone who was "married" to their job, for whom everything and everyone, including family, was a distant second to career? If, as this chapter argues, work is what we were created for, how do you maintain a proper balance between your work life, your family, and other obligations?

3. Read Proverbs 6:6-11; 12:27; 13:4; 20:4; 21:25-26; 22:13; 24:30-34; 26:13-16; Matthew 25:24-30; Ephesians 4:28; 1 Thessalonians 4:10-12; 2 Thessalonians 3:6-12; 1 Timothy 5:8, 13. What do these verses tell us about how we should work? Is that how you work in your current calling?

4. Have you ever considered the idea that God worked in creating the world? What do you think of the idea that God deliberately left the creation incomplete for us to bring it to its final state in the City of God? How does that idea affect the way you view your work and your activities?

5. What is the connection between work and property rights? Medieval theologians argued that the right to property predated government and thus could not be violated by government (except for taxation to pay for its legitimate functions). Do you agree that property rights are unalienable? Does anyone have a right to the fruit of other people's work? Why or why not?

6. What is the relationship between work and the themes discussed in previous chapters such as stewardship, creativity, and reason?

The Image of God

N I N E

THE IMAGE OF GOD
AND SCIENCE

AGENTS AND REPRESENTATIVES

As we have seen in earlier chapters, the image of God refers
primarily to humanity's call to be God's regents and representatives on Earth—to be His stewards. To equip us to carry out
this task, God built a number of unique abilities into humanity, including creativity and reason. We have seen how these
are used in our calling to physical labor as we "tend and take
care of the garden" (Gen. 2:15); these same abilities also come
into play as we engage in intellectual work, as Adam did when
God called him to name the animals (Gen. 2:19-20).

The task of naming the animals is much more involved
than it sounds. In Hebrew, a being's name is supposed to
reflect its nature. In order to give the animals their proper
names, Adam needed first to study them to understand their
natures. Understanding the natural world is a vital part of
our mandate to govern it as God's stewards, of course, and
not surprisingly, there are other examples of observation of
nature in Scripture. Many Psalms talk about the natural world
and relate it back to divine wisdom and God as creator and
sustainer of all things (e.g. Ps. 104); other Psalms and passages tell us that the creation speaks to us and teaches us about
God (e.g. Ps. 19, Rom. 1:18-23). Many of Jesus' parables are

drawn from nature as well. Wisdom—the practical application of divine knowledge—includes knowledge of the natural world. Solomon's wisdom included not only proverbs and judgments, but understanding trees and plants, mammals, birds, reptiles, and fish (1 Kings 4:33).

A MANDATE FOR SCIENCE

To put it differently, just as the mandate to tend the garden implies economic and artistic production and the creation of culture, so the mandate to name the animals is a mandate for us to do science.

It is very common today for people to treat science and religion as if they were two completely separate, unconnected spheres. Science, it is argued, deals with the world of cold, hard facts; religion deals with "spiritual" things, morality, and areas of faith, not knowledge. Yet in fact, this is a false dichotomy. Science may focus on the physical world, but the entire enterprise is based on assumptions about the nature of the world and the nature of humanity that are anything but provable by scientific means. Any apparent conflict between science and religion comes from exactly how those assumptions are set up.

For a Christian, the critical assumptions that enable us to do science are simple. God is rational, and so the world He created is rational. Human beings are made in God's image and thus we are also rational. As a result, even if we cannot understand everything God did exhaustively, we can to some extent "think God's thoughts after Him" and discover the rational processes ("laws") that govern the physical universe.

CULTURAL CONTRASTS

This line of reasoning may seem obvious to us, but that is because our thinking has been firmly shaped by the Christian worldview. The reason modern science arose in the West is because Christianity provided the necessary intellectual framework for it to develop. Medieval theologians working in what was then known as natural philosophy or natural theology laid a foundation for the later scientific revolution, which itself was led by men such as Copernicus, Kepler, Galileo, Pascal, and Newton, all of whom were serious Christians firmly grounded in biblical ideas about God and the creation.

Contrast this with other cultures. In many Asian systems of thought, the world is a kind of illusion or dream in the mind of God. In Islam, Allah has direct control of everything that happens, and in medieval Islam the idea of natural law was seen by many as apostasy because such laws would limit Allah's freedom. In pagan and animistic cultures, the world is largely sentient and is about as predictable as human behavior. None of these provides a solid enough foundation for the development of science (in the sense of empirically backed explanations of why the physical world works as it does).

And then there's secularism, and particularly scientism—the idea that the natural sciences provide the only reliable route to knowledge.

SCIENTISM

Scientism typically posits that the universe somehow came into existence, then by the laws of physics galaxies, stars, and solar systems formed; on at least one planet organic compounds came into existence by the same laws of physics; somehow these organic compound spontaneously generated life (a process which never happens again), and then by random mutation this earliest form of life turned into human beings with brains capable of understanding the universe.

Yet under these circumstances, it is a leap of faith to believe that the universe is understandable or that our minds can in fact make sense of it. If our brains are the product of random mutation and chemical reactions, why would we assume they could comprehend anything reliably?[1]

Further, as Alvin Plantinga points out, the most that undi-

1   http://www.breakpoint.org/features-columns/ articles/999-is-christianity -the-enemy-of-science

rected evolution would do is to give us minds that are geared for survival, not necessarily for discovering truth. While we might think that true ideas enhance survivability, this is not necessarily so. People may behave in a way that helps them survive even if the reasoning that leads to the behavior is false. Plantinga's example is a man named Paul, who, upon encountering a tiger runs away. He may do this because he does not want to be eaten, but there are other possible reasons as well: he may *want* to be eaten, but doesn't think this particular tiger will do it; or he may think the tiger's a big pussy cat and want to pet it, but thinks the best way to get the cat to let him is to run from it; or he might think he is in a race and the tiger's appearance is the signal for him to start. It doesn't matter what he believes or why, just so long as he runs. In other words, his survival does not prove the truth of his belief system. And this means that if both evolution and naturalism (that is, the idea that the natural world of matter and energy are all that exists) are true, we cannot rely on our minds to come to true conclusions, thus rendering all of science irrational.[2]

So even though a purely secular worldview based on naturalism might *seem* to be the best basis for doing science, on closer examination it isn't. Scientism is a logically self-defeating position. It only seems plausible because it is living off the borrowed capital of the biblical worldview, that rational human beings can make sense of the rational universe—because both were made by a rational God.

The biblical teachings about God, the physical world, and human nature thus provide the firmest foundation for science of any competing worldview. But even more, in the command to name the animals, God implicitly commands us to study and to come to understand the natural world as part of the work He has given us. This makes science an essential element

2   See http://www.calvin.edu/academic/philosophy/ virtual_library/articles/plantinga_alvin/naturalism_defeated.pdf for an outline of Plantinga's "Evolutionary Arguments against Naturalism," and his book *Warrant and Proper Function* (New York: Oxford University Press, 1993).

of our stewardship of the world. It shows us something of God's amazing understanding, wisdom and power, helps us understand Him and his ways better, and enables us to develop the resources He has given us in the world in the best ways we can to the glory of God.

QUESTIONS

1. What do you think is the relationship between science and religion? Can they work together? If so, how?

2. Our culture often claims directly or indirectly that science and religion are in conflict, and when there is a conflict, religion must give way to science. Can you think of any examples of this?

3. What are some of the core ideas within Christianity that make it possible to do science? Why is doing science important for the Christian?

4. For centuries some, called Deists, have believed that, after God created the cosmos, He left it alone. For them, prayer is of no use because God has left His creation to work out its fate on its own. The Bible, however, is full of examples of God's continuing concern, intervention and sustaining love. What do you think? Is prayer worthwhile, or does everything in the universe occur by natural cause and effect? In other words, can science explain everything that happens, or can there be supernatural causes of natural events?

5. This chapter argues that taken on its own terms, "scientism" and the belief that matter and energy are all that exists effectively make it impossible to be consistent and to do science. Explain the argument. Do you agree or disagree? Why?

6. Read Ps. 9. In the middle ages, theologians often talked about two books written by God, the book of nature and the book of Scripture. Both required study to be properly understood and each helped illuminate the other. What does the "speech" you hear from the heavens tell you?

7. Read Ps. 104 and Rom. 1:18-32. What are some of the lessons we should learn from the creation?

T E N

THE IMAGE OF GOD
AND FREE WILL

MAKING CHOICES?

One of the most important aspects of the image of God is our ability to make choices. Without this, creativity disappears, reason is reduced to mathematical calculations, work becomes robotic, and our role as God's regents in the world is reduced to being an automaton. Freedom—the ability to make choices—is thus an essential element of what it means to be human.

Free will is under attack today from thinkers who reject the idea that humanity has a non-physical side, a "ghost in the machine." Naturalism (also called materialism)—the premise that the physical world of matter and energy is all that exists—has no room for anything beyond our physical bodies that can make "free" choices, and thus naturalists routinely deny free will. At the same time, however, they also insist that we can know right and wrong and thus are morally responsible, and that we are "causal agents" and thus not bound by rigid determinism.[1]

And yet, what is the "we" that makes us "causal agents?" To a naturalist, the "we" is simply a consequence of chemical processes in the brain, processes which themselves are the product of other chemical processes, and ultimately of physical

---

1   See, for example, http://www.naturalism.org/ roundup.htm#2010.

laws. To the naturalist, matter and energy are all that exists, and their behavior is governed by the laws of science, which can never be violated. Thus everything about us, including our brain chemistry, is unchangeable since it is governed by the inviolable laws of science. A consistent naturalist thus has to argue we are nothing more than products of physical laws, that consciousness, free will, "causal agency," and moral responsibility are nothing more than illusions, epiphenomena of chemical processes which determine our thoughts but over which we have no control and can set no direction other than what has been predetermined by the laws of biochemistry.

Ultimately, this is a dead end road, because it means we cannot even rely on our minds to make rational decisions, since our reason itself is nothing more than electrochemical reactions produced by our brain chemistry.

THE BIBLICAL VIEW OF FREEDOM

In contrast, the Bible teaches that our thoughts, our desires, our values, and our choices all have meaning, and that we have genuine freedom to make decisions and to act accordingly. It is this freedom that allowed Adam to decide how to tend the garden and develop culture, to choose names for the animals, and ultimately to make the moral choice about whether or not to follow God's instructions with respect to the Tree of the Knowledge of Good and Evil.

But how does free will work? If the naturalist is wrong in thinking the mind is only a matter of brain chemistry, then what is free will and how does it fit into the biblical picture of humanity?

It needs to be said at the outset that there is no clear answer to this question, and so a complete explanation of free will is impossible. Perhaps the easiest entry point to understanding free will is through a variation on the medieval theologians' ideas of "faculty psychology." This view held that the mind (broadly understood) was separate from the body and consisted of a number of distinct "faculties" that were independent but interacted with each other. The original list was long: intelligence, perception, memory, will, etc. In the eighteenth and nineteenth century, the number was reduced to three: emotions, will, and intellect, roughly corresponding to the biblical categories of heart, soul, and mind.

THE DIALOGUE OF THE SOUL

Heart, soul, and mind are constantly influencing each other. The will or soul (Greek *psyche*, the root word for psychology) chooses what the conscious mind will dwell on. What the mind focuses on creates a track that it can follow with increasing ease, and these ideas eventually makes their way into the subconscious, which is part of the domain of the heart. The heart uses the input from the mind to form desires and attachments. These desires then inform the will/soul, which then directs the mind to think even more about those desires. The heart can even bypass the will to some extent (if we aren't paying attention) and encourage the conscious mind directly to continue dwelling on the things it desires.

This dynamic explains the instructions in the Bible for dealing with our mental life. Phil. 4:8 tells us that we are to think about the things that are true, honorable, just, pure, lovely, commendable, excellent, and worthy of praise—which implies that we need to make a choice to do so rather than to allow our minds to just drift or to dwell on other things. Again, what we think about habitually shapes our hearts. And Prov. 4:23 exhorts us to guard our heart, because from it flow the issues of life. The heart, the subconscious mind, is the seat of our deepest desires and is therefore the motivating force behind nearly everything we do. And we guard our heart by refusing to allow our minds on things to dwell on things that do not promote trust in God and by focusing on those that do (e.g. Phil. 4:6-7).

What all this means is that while we do have freedom to make choices, those choices are not random coin tosses—they are conditioned by our hearts' desires, "the weight of our love," as St. Augustine put it.

MAKING MORAL CHOICES

Our ability to weigh options and make choices based on what we value enables us to prioritize, to decide how to use our time, to do meaningful work, to decide what to order at a restaurant. Most importantly, however, it also enables us to make moral choices.

For an action to be morally meaningful, it has to be freely chosen. Many naturalists deny this connection, but the claim that our actions have moral significance is meaningless in the face of the naturalist's view that we are nothing more than biochemical machines. All our thoughts and actions are the products of physics and chemistry, making us little more than robots that have only the illusion of independent action. Under these circumstances, it is hard to make a credible claim that our actions are morally meaningful.[2]

The importance of freedom for morality means that a person must be able to choose to act either morally or immorally in a given situation. As we have seen, however, our choices, made by our will, are conditioned by the state of the heart and the "weight of our love." If we love goodness, we will choose the good; if we love something else more than goodness, we will choose that.

So our moral actions depend on freedom, but that freedom in turn is governed by our hearts. This is why Jesus tells us that if we love Him, we will obey His commandments (Jn. 14:15, 21): our love determines our actions. Similarly, this connection between what we love and our actions explains why Jesus tells us that the greatest commandment is to love God with all our heart, soul, mind, and strength, and the second to love our neighbor as ourselves (Matt. 22:37-40). Or as Paul puts it, love is the fulfillment of the Law (Rom. 13:10).

Taking this idea of freedom beyond the personal level, we

---

2   Considering the naturalist also rejects the idea that good and evil have any independent existence, it is unclear what would "morally meaningful" means in a naturalist system.

also see that God is vitally concerned with freeing us from bondage of all kinds. The centerpiece of Israel's identity was God's act of freeing them from slavery in Egypt with the Exodus; the Mosaic Law ordered that Israelite slaves be set free every seventh year; Jesus came to free us from our bondage to sin; the early Christians even went to Roman slave markets to purchase slaves for the specific purpose of setting them free. Freedom is a central element of the biblical story, and it is therefore not surprising that medieval theologians identified liberty as an inalienable right, given by God to all people and thus out of the reach of human authorities. Thomas Aquinas even identified slavery as sin.

Human freedom is thus an important part of the Bible's message, and a critical element of the image of God. Unfortunately, the freedom to do good also means the freedom to choose the not-good instead. In the next chapter, we will explore what the choice not to do good means for the image of God that we bear.

QUESTIONS

1. Have you encountered anyone who denied free will? If so, on what basis did they do so? How do you respond to their arguments?

2. Why is freedom so important for carrying out our responsibilities as people created in the image of God? What are the different areas of life influenced by free will?

3. Lord Acton said, "Liberty is not the power of doing what we like, but the right of being able to do what we ought." Do you agree with him? Why or why not? Are there right and wrong uses of freedom?

4. By our free will, we can choose to do both positive and negative actions. We all want to do right, of course, but often we don't. When you are tempted and you fail, what kinds of considerations led you to choose to do wrong?

5. In his essay, "Men without Chests,"[3] C. S. Lewis talks about the battle between reason ("the head") and "mere appetites" ("the belly"). He argues that reason stands no chance in this battle without "the chest," which he describes as the seat of "emotions organized by *trained habit* into stable sentiments" (emphasis added). What can you do to develop the "trained habits" that build your "chest" so that you can control your appetites and impulses?

6. Read John 8:31-36. How does knowing truth bring us freedom? What does sin do to our free will? Read Rom. 6:16-23. Which is true freedom, following our own desires even if they lead us to sin, or obeying Christ? Do you agree with Paul? What are the consequences of each choice?

---

3   http://www.columbia.edu/cu/augustine/arch/lewis/abolition1.htm.

E L E V E N

The Image of God
and the Fall

The Gift of Freedom

As we have seen in previous chapters, when God created humanity He gave us a tremendous privilege and responsibility to act as His stewards in the world, as well as amazing gifts to empower us to complete the work He gave us of developing the earth, creating culture, and bringing to completion the work that He began. Among those gifts was free will.

Human freedom is essential if we are to carry out God's purposes in producing culture. God does not want automatons, so He gave us the gift of freedom and creativity and the scope to exercise our gifts under His authority. Even more, freedom is necessary for us to develop as persons who reflect God's own character. God wants us to be virtuous, but that means that we must have the freedom not to act virtuously. If the potential for vice does not exist, we cannot be praised for being virtuous. Similarly, God wants us to love Him, but love that is coerced is not love. Love must be freely given or it is not love. So to be the people that God wants us to be, as well as to carry out the work He made us to do, we must be free.

A Test Failed

The Bible tells us in Gen. 2 that God placed Adam and Eve

in the Garden of Eden and provided everything they needed to flourish: abundant food, close companionship, meaningful work, an open relationship with Him. He only placed one restriction on them: they could not eat the fruit of the Tree of the Knowledge of Good and Evil (Gen. 2:17),[1] because on the day they did, they would die. Here was a test of obedience, self-restraint, trust, and love, with clear consequences for disobedience.

We failed comprehensively.

It started off with the serpent getting Eve to doubt God (Gen. 3:1-4). The "ice breaker" question was whether they could eat any fruit at all, to which Eve replied they could, except for the fruit of one tree—and then she went beyond what God told her by saying they could not eat it *or touch it* or they would die. Eve's first mistake was a Pharisaical misinterpretation of the commandment that prohibited more than was commanded. Then the serpent outright called God a liar and questioned His love for Adam and Eve and concern for their well-being, suggesting that God was keeping something from them out of His own self-interest. Thus deceived, Eve began to think about the fruit: it was visually appealing and edible, the two key characteristics of the trees in the Garden, and so she decided to eat it. Not only that, but she gave some to Adam as well (Gen. 3:6).

Adam knew full well that what they were doing was wrong—he wasn't deceived by the serpent—but knowingly and intentionally decided to disobey anyway. John Milton in *Paradise Lost* suggests that Adam did this because he couldn't stand the thought of losing Eve, and thus "completed" the first sin that his wife had begun. Whatever his motive, however, Adam's action sealed the deal: they had betrayed God first by lack of trust in His goodness and love, by doubt of His word, by believing the deceiving serpent more than God, and finally by open rebellion.

---

1 It was not an apple. That idea came from a Latin pun: the word for "evil" is *malus* and the word for "apple tree" is *mālus*. When the pun got translated into popular culture (and the vernacular), it was taken literally.

RESULTS OF THE FALL

The results were disastrous. The first and obvious one was shame (Gen. 3:7) and an effort to cover over what they had done by using their creativity to fashion clothes of fig leaves. Their open relationship with God was broken, so that they hid from Him out of shame and quite likely fear of the consequences of their actions (Gen. 3:8). When God graciously sought them out and tried to coax a confession from them, we see that sin not only resulted in psychological damage to them individually, but shattered the unity that Adam and Eve had previously enjoyed in their marriage. Adam put the blame on Eve *and on God Himself*: "the woman *you put here with me*—she gave me the some fruit" (Gen. 3:12). For her part, Eve blamed the serpent (Gen. 3:13).

And so God pronounced His judgment. The serpent was cursed to live in the dust, to unending hostility with Eve and her offspring, and ultimately to death at the hand of the "seed of the woman" (Gen. 3:14-15), a topic to which we will return in the next chapter.

BLESSINGS LOST

Neither Eve nor Adam was cursed directly. For Eve, God's blessing was turned to a source of suffering. Prior to this, blessing was always associated with "being fruitful and multiplying;" now, Eve would experience pain in childbirth. Further, her relationship with Adam changed. Rather than the equality between the two that existed prior to this, Eve was now in the difficult position of "desiring" him—a reference to her sexuality and thus her inability to escape the first part of her judgment, as well as to her desire for the kind of psychological and emotional intimacy that had been lost—but also became subordinated to him so that he would now "rule" over her the way they had together "ruled" over the other creatures (Gen. 3:16).[2] As a

2   This is not God's intent for marriage or a command about how things should be; it is a statement of what would follow. In the New Testament teaching about marriage, we see a restoration of much of the equality and mutuality that prevailed before the Fall.

result, "the woman" (as she is known up to this point) is given a new name by Adam and only now becomes known as "Eve" (meaning "living"), since she would be the source of all subsequent human life (Gen. 3:20). Adam "naming" her may also be an indication of his "rule" over her after the Fall.

For Adam, the curse fell on the earth itself. As God's steward, it was Adam's responsibility and privilege to "tend the Garden," growing his food and developing culture; now, what should have been a wonderful and joyful task would turn to drudgery. This struck at the heart of what it meant to bear the image of God and to a critical element of man's self-identity. Just as Eve's role as the bearer of children was now filled with suffering, so the work necessary to fulfilling Adam's purpose became tainted with frustration and struggle. In fact, the same word "pain" is used to describe Eve's pain in childbirth and Adam's labor. Moreover, the prospect of death enters the picture, as God reminds Adam that he would return to the dust from which he had been taken (Gen. 3:17-19).

And so in Gen. 3, we see sin breaking our fellowship with God, creating psychological problems within ourselves, striking at the heart of our families and our most intimate relationships, bringing pain into childbearing and struggle and frustration into our work, and even damaging our bodies. But all of this is only the tip of the iceberg. Sin affects every part of our being. It corrupts the desires of our hearts so that we do not want the things we should; since our desires form our will, we choose to do the wrong rather than the right; our corrupted hearts also blind our reason so that we refuse to see what is plain to us about God and the moral order (Rom. 1:18-32) and lead us to use our creativity to devise ways to do evil.[3] Like Eve we do not trust God enough to obey Him, and like Adam we openly defy Him.

---

3   This is what Calvinists mean when they talk about "Total Depravity," not that we are as bad as we could be, but that every aspect of our being is affected by sin.

ORIGINAL SIN AND THE PROBLEM OF SIN

Because of the sin of our primordial parents, we all have "original sin," that is, an inborn tendency to disobey God. To understand this, consider different breeds of dogs: some are natural hunters and have behaviors bred into them that enhance their ability to do this well; others are hopeless as hunters but amazing as herding dogs, again with different sets of behaviors they inherit from their ancestors. Just as dogs have been bred for specific behaviors, so are we. Only in our case, we've been bred to sin. Thus Seth, the progenitor of the *godly* line after the Fall, is described not as the image of God as Adam had been, but as the image of Adam (Gen. 5:2-3), indicating Adam's sin had been passed down to him.

But the problem of sin is even bigger than that. Since we are the image of God, His representatives and regents on earth, even the natural world has been affected by human sin so that it cannot fulfill the purposes which God intended for it (Rom. 8:20-22). Our failure means that God's intent for the world to be developed, for the Garden of Eden to become the City of God, was delayed and even threatened.

But God's will cannot be thwarted. Even though Adam's offspring were in his fallen and sinful image, the image of God was not lost—it was marred, but it was not completely effaced. Even after the Flood, God affirmed to Noah that human beings were all made in His image (Gen. 9:6). So we remain God's regents here, even though this is a much more painful and difficult job to do so since we have to fight not just the cursed ground but our own nature as well.

Further, God had His contingency plans in place for Adam's disobedience. Though Adam was reminded of his mortality, he did not die on the day He ate the fruit. But something did: God Himself replaced the fig leaves with clothes made from animal skins for Adam and Eve (Gen. 3:21). Our parents' guilt and shame was covered by an animal that died so they wouldn't have to—a substitutionary sacrifice for their sin that pointed the way ahead to the time that the seed of the woman would destroy the serpent but be wounded Himself in the process (Gen. 3:17). We will examine that in more detail in our next chapter.

QUESTIONS

1. This chapter argues that you cannot have virtue without the potential for vice, and thus that free will automatically creates the potential for evil. Do you agree? Why or why not? What is the difference between that statement and the idea that you cannot have good without evil?

2. Read Rom. 5:12-14. According to this passage, what is the relationship between Adam's sin and our own? Original sin is a very controversial idea in some circles. Does this passage support the idea of original sin? Why or why not?

3. How much of an effect does sin have within us? Does it influence all parts of our being, as Calvinists teach?

4. Trappist monk Thomas Merton wrote, "One of the effects of original sin is an instinctive prejudice in favour of our own selfish desires. We see things as they are not, because we see them centered on ourselves. Fear, anxiety, greed, ambition and our hopeless need for pleasure all distort the image of reality that is reflected in our minds." Where do you see people distorting reality in favor of their own preferred view of the world? Can you identify any ways in which you do this yourself?

5. People frequently argue that crime is caused by poverty, social conditions, or other unfavorable circumstances in life. What does the story of the Fall in Genesis 3 suggest about these explanations of crime? What do you think causes criminal behavior?

6. Can we be good without God? Why or why not?

THE IMAGE OF GOD

T W E L V E

THE IMAGE OF GOD
AND JESUS THE CHRIST

IMAGE BEARERS IN SPITE OF THE FALL

Adam and Eve's fall into sin had immediate and devastating effects on their relationship with God (hiding and separation), with each other (blame and recrimination) and with themselves (shame and guilt). The judgment which followed struck at the heart of God's blessing to them (pain in childbirth) and of His mandate to tend the garden and develop culture (pain in work); it also made this a lifelong sentence, to end only with death.[1] Nonetheless, Adam and Eve's responsibility to act as God's steward was not taken away: they and their descendants continued to be God's image-bearers. Now, however, their job would be infinitely harder.

In the midst of the devastation brought about by sin and judgment, however, we have a word of hope. God told the serpent: "And I will put enmity Between you and the woman, And between your seed and her seed; He shall bruise you on the head, And you shall bruise him on the heel." (Gen. 3:15 NAS) This promise, known as the *protoevangelium* ("first Gospel"), points to a day when the "seed of the woman"

---

1   This is one reason Adam and Eve were expelled from the Garden: to keep them from eating from the Tree of Life and never dying. In a world of suffering and change, natural death and an end to toil and pain can be a mercy.

would deliver a fatal blow to the serpent but would himself be wounded in the process. Over the Old Testament Scripture, the seed of the woman would be narrowed down to the seed of Abraham, of Isaac, of Jacob, of Judah, and of David; we learn in Isaiah that the promise would be fulfilled by the child of a virgin, who would be God with us. Ultimately, all of these promises and prophecies were fulfilled in Jesus, the child of a virgin mother, "who was born of a descendant of David according to the flesh, who was declared the Son of God with power by the resurrection from the dead, according to the Spirit of holiness...." (Rom 1:3b-4a)

In other words, giving Adam and Eve free will ultimately involved the risk that they would disobey God's commands and thus throw the world into chaos. But God was ready for their sin, and put in motion a plan He had in place even from before the foundation of the world (cf. Rev. 13:8). And the scope of that plan is nothing short of breathtaking.

GOD'S ETERNAL PLAN IN JESUS

First, Jesus dealt with our guilt. God had told Adam that on the day he ate the fruit of the Tree of the Knowledge of Good and Evil, he would die. Spiritually, he did, but not physically: God provided a substitute, an animal that died to provide the skins that would cover Adam and Eve's shame. Here we have the first substitutionary sacrifice, pointing ahead to the sacrificial system of the Law and ultimately to Jesus' death on the cross, whereby he delivered the death blow to Satan and was himself wounded in the process. All of the earlier sacrifices from Eden on were pictures of the coming sacrifice of Jesus, whose death finally and definitively paid in full the debt we owe to God for our disobedience.

In order for Jesus' death to be effective for us, however, He needed to be sinless Himself. And for that He needed, like Adam, to be born without the taint of original sin dragging

Him down.[2] He had to be, in essence, a new Adam, one who faced the test of obedience but who remained faithful in the midst of that testing. He also experienced the full brunt of suffering in this world and God's judgment on Adam—He worked as a skilled craftsman; he experienced hunger, thirst, and exhaustion; He was misunderstood and slandered, rejected, betrayed by those closest to Him, mocked, tortured, and killed. But through it all He never lost His trust in God and never wavered in His obedience and submission to God's will.

And as if that were not enough, He rose from the dead, His transformed body a paradigm for the bodies His followers will receive at the resurrection. But even in this world, the resurrection matters: Jesus' death broke the hold of sin and death over our lives, and the resurrection then gives us new life and the power to live in obedience to the calling God has given us. We participate in the Great Exchange: Jesus takes our guilt, and we take His righteousness; Jesus takes our punishment, and we receive His reward; Jesus suffers death for us, and we receive His life in this world and the next.

And all this is predicated on faith and trust—the very place where Adam and Eve failed. In essence, we get what we place our trust in: if we trust Christ, we receive what He deserves; if we trust in ourselves, we get what we deserve. If we trust in Christ, we get His power to live the way we were made to live; if we trust ourselves, we're on our own.

THE NEW ADAM

So Jesus is truly the new Adam (1 Cor. 15:45, cf. Rom. 5:12-21), the progenitor of a new humanity that is redeemed from guilt, delivered from death, and empowered to carry out God's mission and purposes in this world.

But there's still more: Col. 1:15 tells us that Jesus "... is the image of the invisible God, the firstborn of all creation." Humanity was made in the image of God and continues to

---

2   This probably has something to do with the virgin birth, though how exactly sin is transmitted is not explained in Scripture.

bear it, but Jesus is preeminently the image of God, the one who is God's definitive representative on Earth, who speaks with God's voice and authority, who is quite literally the face of God on Earth—the fullness of deity in bodily form (vs. 19). As the firstborn of creation,[3] Jesus is the heir of all things, the means by which everything came into existence and the one who holds everything together, as Col. 1:15-20 explain. This makes him preeminent over the created order, the one who fully exercises the dominion given to humanity. Salvation is thus truly cosmic in scope: John 3:16 tells us that God loved the *cosmos*, the ordered world that was subject to futility because of human sin (Rom. 8:20). And just as the bodies of the redeemed will be transformed at the resurrection, so will the creation as God brings forth a new heavens and earth where righteousness dwells (1 Pet. 3:13).

Until then, we are living in a new reality in this world. Sin may have marred the image of God and made our mandate to "tend and keep the Garden" under God's authority far more difficult, but in Christ the power of sin over our lives has been broken. We are thus freer than we have been since Adam to fulfill God's original calling to humanity, to act as His stewards in all that we do in the world. Our redemption in Christ restores to us the ability to fulfill the cultural mandate that God gave Adam and never revoked. As we carry out the Great Commission and make disciples for Jesus, the image of God and our sovereign king, we are actually to be calling people not just to Heaven, but to live out the Lordship of Christ in every area of their lives and thus to fulfill our original calling on Earth.

---

3   "Firstborn" is not always literal in Scripture; it also refers to someone who is an heir (whether the firstborn or not) or someone who is preeminent in some way. Given the following verses, it is clear that Paul is not describing Jesus as the first created being but rather as the one who is preeminent over all creation, including the spiritual world.

QUESTIONS

1. What is your understanding of the Gospel? Is it just about forgiveness of sins, or is it more than that?

2. What does it mean that Christ is the "new Adam?" How does he fulfill the role of the first Adam? Review the discussion of the image of God in the previous chapters. How does Jesus fulfill the different facets we've examined?

3. Why is Jesus' resurrection important? What affect does it have on our lives today? In the future?

4. Read Col. 1:15-20. What things beside our salvation does this passage teach you about Jesus' work?

5. In the hymn "Joy to the World," Isaac Watts wrote:

   No more let sins and sorrows grow
   Nor thorns infest the ground.
   He comes to make His blessings flow
   Far as the curse is found.

   Do you see the work of Christ as extending "far as the curse is found?" How far does the curse extend? How does the work of Christ reach to all of those areas?

6. When you think of Jesus, how do you picture him? Read Rev. 1:13-18. How does this affect how you think of Jesus?

7. The distractions of this world often make it hard to give our creator God appropriate honor and credit. But when we do fully recognize all that we owe Christ, then we should be on fire with love for and appreciation of God in Jesus, and Jesus should be the center of our lives. Is this true of you? Or have you yet to truly put Jesus at the center of your life?

THIRTEEN

The Image of God

THE IMAGE OF GOD
AND RESTORATION

ALIENATED

The fall into sin had devastating effects on Adam and Eve
both as a direct consequence of their disobedience and in the
judgment by God which followed. We see in Gen. 3 sin producing alienation from God (Adam and Eve hid from Him),
from ourselves (feelings of shame), from our neighbor (Adam
blames Eve, and the relationship between husband and wife is
terribly distorted), and ultimately from the natural world (the
ground is cursed to produce thorns and thistles rather than
yielding its bounty to Adam's labor).

Given the incredible range of effects of sin, God's recovery
plan had to be able to deal comprehensively with all of these
problems. Redemption in Christ is thus much bigger than simply dealing with the guilt of our sin and restoring our relationship with God. It also provides the means for dealing with the
consequences of the Fall in this life.

A FIRM FOUNDATION

Psychologically, many (though by no means all) of our problems stem from guilt—on this, Freud had a valid point. Where
Freud went wrong is in failing to recognize that guilt isn't just
a matter of feelings; rather, true moral guilt also exists and is

the source of many of our guilty feelings. Pop psychology has followed Freud in denying the reality of guilt and trying to free people from *feeling* guilty without ever recognizing the underlying problem that we actually are guilty. But because pop psychology has no means of dealing with true guilt, it can never truly solve our psychological problems.

The Good News is that in Christ, our guilt is taken away through the Cross. As a result, we don't need to hide from guilt or deny it—in fact, we must acknowledge and confess it, agreeing with God about His evaluation of our behavior but also trusting in Christ to bear our guilt and shame. This gives us a firm foundation for dealing with our true guilt as well as our feelings of guilt and shame at our behavior—God knows all about it, and He has accepted and forgiven us anyway. While we need to mourn our sin and repent of it, we do not need to allow it to paralyze us anymore.

Restored Relationships

Christianity also did much to restore relationships between people who were often hostile to each other. Early Christians insisted that all people were spiritually and morally equal before God. This led to a very different ethic among early Christians in keeping with Jesus' commands to love our enemies and pray for those who persecute us (Matt. 5:44) and to love our neighbors as ourselves (Matt. 22:39), as well as Paul's teaching about humility (Phil. 2:1-4) and about Christ demolishing the dividing wall of hostility between Jews and Gentiles (Eph. 2:14).

The historical consequences of this new view of our equality before God in Christ led Christians to lead in the battle to eliminate slavery, starting with churches and individual Christians in the Roman Empire who purchased slaves for the sole reason of setting them free. The same attitude led Christians to oppose abortion and infanticide, and led the monk Telemachus to try to halt a gladiatorial match at the cost of his own life. Modern ideas of civil equality and human rights also have their roots in Christian thought.

EQUALITY AND RIGHTS

Modern ideas about civil rights and equality also have their roots in Christian thought. In particular, the Christian emphasis on spiritual and moral equality led to a new view of women and a restoration of marriage as a partnership between equals. As we have seen, the Woman was originally made as an equal of the Man, though it seems that the Man was to be the leader in the relationship (as indicated by his naming the Woman in Gen. 2:23). This proper relationship was distorted by the Fall, with the subjugation of women following as the result of sin. This type of subjugation was a central element of Greco-Roman culture, as was pervasive misogyny.

In contrast, Paul taught that we are all to be subject to each other for the love of Christ: wives are subject to husbands, and husbands are to love their wives as Christ loved us: He looked out for our interests rather than His own and laid down His life for us (Eph. 5:21-33). The role of the husband is thus transformed into a servant leader who has no right to insist on his way but who must self-sacrificially serve his wife. This new attitude also gave women new rights and status within Christian communities, as documented by Rodney Stark.[1]

THE HARMONY OF CREATION

The coming of Christ also begins the process of restoring the harmony of the natural world, as prophesied in the Peaceful Kingdom passage (Is. 11:6-9) and in promises of the desert blooming and flowing with water (e.g. Is. 35:1-2, 6-7). While the full restoration of Creation to its proper functioning awaits the Second Coming, in the meantime Christians have historically called for responsible stewardship of resources on the one hand, and have worked to mitigate the effects of the Fall on our labor on the other.

---

1   See The Rise of Christianity, 95-128.

WORK AND TECHNOLOGY

As we have seen, God intended work to be good, but sin turned it into drudgery. Not surprisingly, then, in the ancient world across the globe, work was seen as something fit only for slaves and inferiors. In Christianity, work was restored to an honored place. Paul himself worked (Acts 18:3) and encouraged others to do so (1 Thes. 4:11; 2 Thes. 3:10). For this reason, early monks were commanded to engage in work, both as an exercise in humility and out of obedience to the biblical commands.

But if work is good, drudgery is evil. People should work, but should do so in a way that engages the whole person as much as possible. People shouldn't do the kind of repetitive, mindless work that animals or machines can do just as well—it undermines the intrinsic dignity of work. As a result, the monasteries of the middle ages began an early industrial revolution, harnessing water power to grind grain. The technology was then adapted to full cloth, operate the bellows in foundries and trip hammers in forges, and make paper, among many other tasks. Wind power was similarly harnessed for many of the same tasks as well as for pumping water out of the *polders* in the Netherlands, land reclaimed from the sea for farming.

A host of other technologies also developed in the Christian middle ages, ranging from eye glasses to blast furnaces, horseshoes to spinning wheels, and the effort to produce technologies to improve work and the life of the working classes has continued in the West ever since.

Other cultures had fabulous technologies long before the West began to develop. The difference is that those technologies were never used to develop labor saving devices or to benefit the working class. The Romans, for example, knew about water wheels but never deployed them because they had slaves to do work. The difference was worldview: Christians recognized the dignity of work and the equal dignity of each person. This and this alone provided the motivation for harnessing technology to benefit the workers, not just the elites, and in the process laid the economic foundation for the rise of the West.

THE SCIENTIFIC REVOLUTION

On another front, Christians developed the scientific method and were at the heart of the scientific revolution because they recognized the divine mandate to study the world (chapter 9), and knew that the world was made by a rational God and must therefore be rational itself. Learning about the world meant studying it as it is, because only through that would the mind of God be revealed.

The examples of the impact of Christianity can be multiplied. Although it might not seem that way at first, all of them without exception depend entirely on the work of Christ for their effectiveness. Without the reconciling work of Christ on the Cross, we have no basis for psychological healing, overcoming the differences of race, ethnicity, class, or gender, no power to carry out the mandate God gave us in Adam, and no means of overcoming the curse that our sin laid upon us. But in Christ, all is possible. And as Christians, our part is to continue Christ's work in reversing the curse, working to reconcile our neighbors with God and to bring the blessings of His rule into all areas of life.

QUESTIONS

1. What aspects of the work of Christ discussed here are new to you or are things you have not spent much time considering? Which do you usually hear about or read about?

2. Given the fact that everyone sins, how do you handle your guilt? How do you handle the guilt of people who wrong either you or those close to you? How does Christ's death on the cross affect your response to guilt, including that of those who hurt you?

3. Is there such a thing as universal human rights? If so, where do they come from? How do the truths of the Bible contribute to our understanding of human rights?

4. Read John 17:20-26. What was on Jesus' mind as he was heading into the crucifixion? How have you seen Jesus' work reconcile people across lines that normally divide them—race, class, languages, etc.?

5. Dutch theologian Abraham Kuyper once said,

   ...there is not a square inch in the whole domain of our human existence over which Christ, who is Sovereign over all, does not cry: "Mine!"

   If that is true, what does Christ's sovereignty mean for your job? How does the work of Christ affect your work?

6. Read Rom. 8:19-22. What does it mean that the creation was subject to futility? What does this tell you about the scope of Christ's redemption?

F O U R T E E N

THE IMAGE OF GOD
AND THE CULTURAL MANDATE

GOD'S STEWARDS

To understand fully God's intentions for Christians in this
world, we need to grasp what it means that we are made in
the image of God. As we have seen in earlier chapters, the
term "image of a god" in the ancient near east referred to
someone who was a representative or regent of that god; for
us, it means that our primary identity as human beings is
that we are God's stewards over the world He has made. In
a broad sense, it also includes the gifts and abilities God has
placed in us that enable us to carry out this work, including
gender and marriage, spirituality and physicality, creativity,
rationality, freedom and morality.

Our call as stewards is to continue the work that God
began. He started with a world "without form and void" and
set it in proper order; we are to "tend the Garden," including
both the cultivation of beauty through the arts and the production of food and other necessities. We are also to engage
in the process of learning and discovery through coming to
understand the natural world. And we are to do all of this in
obedience to God, recognizing His authority over the world so
that we cultivate it as stewards, not owners, and do not abuse
His property.

AUTHORITY MISUSED

The reality, however, is that we abused our authority. The story of the Fall points out that we were not willing to live within the limits God placed on us, resulting in broken relationships with God, with each other, with ourselves, and with nature itself. The blessing of children becomes a source of suffering for women, and the blessing of work becomes a source of suffering and frustration for men. Yet neither Adam nor Eve was cursed; children continue to be a blessing and our call as God's regents in the world was never withdrawn. We continue to be God's image, His face in the world, even in our rebellion.

But God had a recovery plan for our disobedience: through the Incarnation of Jesus Christ, the ultimate image of God, through His death, resurrection, and ascension, the penalty due to our sin is paid in full and the power of sin in our lives is broken, thus restoring our relationship with God. This provides a solid foundation for reconciliation with each other and for dealing with the problem of guilt and shame in our own lives. But our redemption in Christ also restores our work and purpose to its proper place. Under the influence of the biblical worldview, the western world developed technologies to eliminate drudgery and to enhance productivity, making western cultures the most prosperous in human history—with both good and bad consequences because of the lingering effect of sin.

WHAT SHALL WE SAY
IN RESPONSE TO THIS?

To put this differently, in Christ, our ability to live out our call as the image of God is restored. Sin isn't gone, but it doesn't have the same hold over us, and we are now free to carry out our mandate to develop culture as stewards of God. This has enormous implications for how we live our lives.

First, it means that Christianity is far more than what most people—including most Christians—think of as "religion" (which typically means little more than religious activities plus morality). Rather, Christianity is a worldview, a vision of the world and our place in it, where every facet of our life—family, occupation, recreation, relationships, finances, *everything*—finds its meaning and end in God's purposes for us and for the world. The Gospel affects all of life, and includes the stewardship of all that God has entrusted to us, whether time, talents, treasure, or relationships.

Second, we need to be active in every sphere of life, and should infuse everything we do with the sure knowledge that we are fulfilling God's call on our lives to be stewards wherever God has placed us. And though we they need to work from the foundation provided by Christ's redemption, we do not necessarily need to wear this on our sleeves. C. S. Lewis once commented that "we don't need more Christian writers, we need more great writers who are Christian." The point is that not everything we do needs to be overtly "Christian." Instead, we need to do whatever we do with excellence, because by so doing we are being good and faithful servants in fulfilling God's purposes for the world. This is what it means that we are to do everything as unto God, not man, and to do it in the name of Christ.

Third, we need to get rid of the idea that only clergy are involved in "full time Christian service." When we understand that all of culture is under God's authority and that He equips each of us to follow our unique calling, it becomes clear that all work should be considered Christian service. Christians in the "secular" sphere are fulfilling God's call to be His stewards by developing culture. To be sure, some are called to vocational ministry as members of the clergy, but their work is no more or less sacred than the business owner or laborer who does her or his work as a calling from God.

Fourth, although evangelism is critically important, it is only the first step for Christians. The Great Commission tells us that wherever we go,[1] we are to make disciples who obey

---

1   The word "go" in the Greek is not a command, it is a participle. The sense is more "in your going" or "as you go" rather than a command to go.

everything that Jesus taught. In other words, we are to make obedient disciples, not converts. Evangelism must lead to discipleship, to teaching people how to live for Jesus in their own walks of life. Jesus only called twelve to be apostles; he left his other disciples in their own professions. We need to learn what it means to be a Christian in our own calling and to help others learn what it means in theirs—and not only in our employment, but in our family, neighborhood, community, and nation, in our friendships, our recreation, even in the care of ourselves. And for this, we need the support and fellowship of other Christians, our fellow members of the body of Christ.

Lastly, to do all of this, we need to catch a vision of why we matter. The entire universe is "the theater of God's glory," as Calvin put it, and yet in this amazing, mysterious, and beautiful universe we occupy a unique place. We alone bridge the gap between time and eternity, matter and spirit, and we have a unique calling to bring to fruition the things God has begun. Each of us is individually designed and equipped to play a key part that only we can do in bringing about God's purposes for His creation. God saved us when we could not save ourselves so that we would carry out the work that He uniquely prepared us to do (Eph. 2:8-10). John 3:16 tells us that God loved the *world* (Greek *cosmos*, the entirety of creation) so much that He gave His son to save those who believe in Him. Our salvation is thus not only for ourselves personally, but for the good of the entire created order.

So let us take up the challenge to live out our identity as God's image on earth, bringing the lordship of Christ to bear in all areas of life, and recognizing that we have a unique and critical role to play, however small it may look to us, in fulfilling God's purposes for the world. And whatever we do, whether in word or deed, let us do it as unto God, not men, in the name of our Lord Jesus Christ.

QUESTIONS

1. This chapter argues that Christians are called and equipped not only to save the lost, but to bring them into the kingdom where we can work together to complete the task God originally gave to Adam in the Garden to build culture. Is this a common view in your Christian circles, or is this a new idea to you? Do you agree or disagree with this understanding of the Gospel? Why?

2. Read Matt. 28:18-20. Has anyone taught you to be a disciple who obeys everything that Jesus taught? Is this something you are doing with others? Is this something your church actively promotes? What can you do to help others to grow as obedient disciples?

3. Make a list of all your roles, relationships, and activities. How central is the lordship of Christ to each of these? Where can you go for help in the areas where you are weak?

4. Modern society has bought into the idea of a division between the sacred and the secular. For the Christian, should there be? How much of this division do you see in your own thinking, in the approach to Christianity in your church, and among your Christian friends?

5. Why is it important to do all our work, whether obviously "Christian" or not, with excellence?

6. What are the most important lessons you have learned from this study of the image of God? What concrete steps are you going to take to incorporate these lessons into your life?

CPSIA information can be obtained at www.ICGtesting.com
Printed in the USA
LVOW10s1333231215

467642LV00005B/237/P